D1029611

p.68!

SELECTED POEMS:
OLD AND NEW

WORKS BY OSBERT SITWELL

Published by Gerald Duckworth & Co. Ltd.

Collected Satires and Poems
Winters of Content
Miracle on Sinai
Dumb Animal
The Man who Lost Himself
Before the Bombardment
England Reclaimed
Discursions on Travel, Art and Life
Triple Fugue
Out of the Flame
Who Killed Cock Robin?
Argonaut and Juggernaut

WITH SACHEVERELL SITWELL
All at Sea

WITH MARGARET BARTON
Sober Truth
Victoriana

WITH NINA HAMNETT
The People's Album of London Statues

Published by Macmillan & Co. Ltd.

Penny Foolish
Mrs. Kimber
Those were the Days
Escape with Me!
Two Generations
A Place of One's Own
Open the Door!
Sing High! Sing Low!
Left Hand, Right Hand! *An autobiography*
 Vol. I. Left Hand, Right Hand!
 Vol. II. The Scarlet Tree
 Vol. III. Great Morning
 Vol. IV. Laughter in the Next Room

WITH R. J. MINNEY
Gentle Caesar

WITH EDITH AND SACHEVERELL SITWELL
Trio: Dissertations on Some Aspects of National Genius

EDITED BY OSBERT SITWELL
A Free House! or The Artist as Craftsman
by WALTER RICHARD SICKERT

SELECTED
POEMS
OLD AND NEW

by

OSBERT SITWELL

DUCKWORTH
3 Henrietta Street
LONDON, W.C.2

First published November 1943
Reprinted 1944 *and* 1949

Printed in Great Britain by The Riverside Press, Edinburgh

DEDICATION

To my brother SACHEVERELL, without whose encouragement these poems would never have been written, and without whose help this book could never have been arranged

My thanks are due to Messrs. Macmillan for allowing me to reprint in the following pages the six poems from *Mrs. Kimber* (Macmillan, 1938)

Preface

IT is not, perhaps, necessary to append a date to each of the poems that follow, but I should state that the first nine poems in this volume have not previously appeared in any book of mine. Among them, *To Charlotte Corday*, *Fool's Song*, first and second, and *Journalist's Song* were the last written, being incidental pieces from an unfinished long poem entitled *Demos The Emperor*. I should add, also, that the poems which these immediately precede are among the earliest. Thus the *Three Mexican Pieces* were composed in 1919, while the *Two Poems from The Phoenix Feasters* appeared originally twenty-five years ago.

Poetic portraiture is a difficult art, one not very often essayed, but the poems reprinted from *England Reclaimed*, published in 1926, were written in an effort to form a gallery of rustic characters, and thus preserve their likeness, and commemorate a tradition and a way of life which were even then fast disappearing and have now vanished. The exigencies of the paper situation have obliged me, however, in this volume, to abbreviate the *Grand Finale*, conceived as a Teniers group of peasants, wherein all the figures which have been introduced separately, re-emerge in a body. I would have preferred to retain the poem in its full form— or to have omitted it altogether, but this could not be done, either, because its exclusion would have forfeited the balance of the whole work, and would have entailed, too, a loss of direction.

Of some of the earlier poems in this book, various members of the public have lately written to me, declaring that they find in them a prophetic quality—but prophecy should always be at poetry's elbow. One reader, for example, calls my attention to the fifth part of *Out of the Flame*, beginning:

> *It is not thus in the Northern cities,*
> *Where the cold breathes close to the window-pane.*

I may say, then, that this sequence was written in 1921, and certainly demonstrates a preoccupation with those problems of poverty and inequality which the extremely gifted, but more politically-minded, poets of the following decade were to seize on as the main theme for their verse. In *Winter the Huntsman*—written in 1924 and published the following year—another reader writes to tell me that he considers I correctly diagnosed the disease from which the world was suffering and detected the future culmination of it. At the time the work appeared this, nevertheless, was not obvious, for though the sequence of poems was written, if I may so phrase it, on two levels, no one seemed then to perceive the substratum. The surface was intended to tell its own story of the seasons; the lower level, of the times in which we lived and whither they were leading us:

> *Is it Winter the Huntsman*
> *Who gallops through his iron glades,*
> *Cracking his cruel whip*
> *To the gathering shades?*

And in the concurrent poems, I certainly tried to show, in the simplest terms applied to the most radical and obvious causes, the reasons, as I saw them, of the plight in which we found ourselves; that religion, intuition, even superstition had been banished from the modern world, and a worship of brute knowledge—science—and of material things had replaced them.

8

For the incense that rises
  Is smoke from a factory.
Though Man now despises
  All flames expiatory,

Yet vast furnaces cast
  Spells, blacker by far
Than those of the past,
  With their 'per cent' and 'par',

And the new race of sombre Man and sullen
  Moans in its sleep and turns,
No trust in Hell or Heaven,
  In fixed star that shines or deep fire that burns.

Similarly, people refused to believe in anything essential, as opposed to the superficial. This attitude I tried to typify in the Countess Klondyke, who

. . . feigned not to hear the bones
That rattled and dangled,
For the glint of the gold
That sparkled and spangled.

For she did not believe
In things which she did not see
—Therefore if she looked the other way
Those things could not be!

Some of the earlier poems, it may be, possess, as well, a period, no less than a prophetic and intrinsic, interest. For instance, the first poem in the fourth book, beginning with the lines:

How shall we rise to greet the dawn,
Not timidly,
With a hand before our eyes,

9

was composed soon after the Armistice, and crystallizes an attitude that, albeit common to-day, will be still more prevalent to-morrow among the young poets. And the satire entitled *Ultimate Judgment* has in the last two years assumed an odd twist, reminding us, as it does, of a time when the Archbishops and Bishops of the Established Church regarded Bolshevism with a degree of horror equal in intensity to their present enthusiasm for it.

Old-Fashioned Sportsmen, again, written just after the First Great War, indicates, through the views put into the mouths of the protagonists, that there were even then men who preferred to attribute the blame for the contemporary conflict to the exponents of modernity in the arts rather than lay it, where it belonged, upon the shoulders of the feeble and verbose politicians. Let us listen: 'Imitations of negro sculpture, engineering diagrams, drawings which suggested the scribbling of children or lunatics, patterns framed upon chance blots or the natural shape of stones, all these followed each other with bewildering rapidity.' Thus our Lord Elton—whom I have heard praise, upon the wireless, the genial virtues of war, as opposed to the horrid sloths of peace—and thus, too, my *Old-Fashioned Sportsmen* of a generation ago:

> *Our sons and brothers*
> *Went forth to fight,*
> *To kill certain things,*
> *Cubism, Futurism and Vers-libre,*
>   *'All this Poetry-and-Rubbish',*
>   *We said,*
>   *'Will not stand the test of war.'*

Of the remaining poems, a rather singular history attaches to that entitled *The Next War*, which was written in November 1918, and published shortly afterwards in the pages of *The Nation*, then edited by Massingham. In 1919, before it had appeared in America, Witter Bynner found this poem, unsigned, scrawled in ink upon the marble top of a table in a café in San Francisco. He was impressed by it, wondered who could be the author, and drew the attention of the newspapers to it. The table-top was photographed and figured in many journals, waiters were interviewed, and the Press started a campaign to try to discover the anonymous writer. Eventually, somehow or other, it was tracked down, and Witter Bynner kindly sent me a letter, enclosing the various newspaper cuttings relative to the affair, and telling me the story of the strange adventures of this poem, starred for months as a piece by an unknown hand. I may add that, unfortunately regaining a certain topicality, *The Next War* was published once more in the pages of the *The Nation and New Statesman* a year or two before the outbreak of the present conflict.

O. S.

Renishaw,
27.iv.43.

Contents

BOOK I

POEMS OLD AND NEW

BOOK II

ENGLAND RECLAIMED

A BOOK OF ECLOGUES AND OTHER PORTRAITS

BOOK III

SATIRES

BOOK IV

POEMS OF THE LAST AND THE NEXT WAR

POEMS OLD AND NEW

I

The Vision

I saw a cloud upon a hill
  Anchor its shadow on a grave;
I saw a Vulture, oh! how still,
  Upon a broken architrave.

I saw a hill within a cloud,
  I saw a grave within its shade;
I saw a Phoenix from its shroud
  Soar upward to a fiery glade.

I saw a man with broken heart
  And angels drooping broken wings;
I heard the rumble of a cart
  Piled up with bodies of dead kings.

And then I saw a cloud ope wide
  And out of it a white dove come,
Alighting in sweet, cooing pride
  Upon the branch that rocked its home.

And then I heard its gentle moan
  Caged in the splendour of the tree,
A sail, a floating cloud held down
  By bird and butterfly and bee.

And then I heard a human voice,
  Far off, in laughter, loud and free;
The Phoenix cried 'Rejoice! Rejoice!'
  And all my soul burned inwardly.

For as she cried, the West Wind blew
   With force gigantic that space gives,
And deep within my heart I knew
   That tyrants die, but freedom lives.

    .   .   .   .

I saw the cloud lift, drift along
   To shelter all the sweltering plains
Whence rose the loud triumphant song
Of broken hearts that break their chains.

I saw the Vulture's scaly face,
   I saw it quit the architrave;
I saw the Phoenix give it chase
   And blossoms burst forth from the grave.

March 1939

2   *To Charlotte Corday*

Oh, Huntsman, when will the hunting stop;
  And the spring begin;
And the first star-eyed blossoms
Sprinkle earth's dull skin,
And Man's sorrow be again
Of divine ordination,
Not this evil, dull fruit
Of Man's negation?

In all lands under wide skies found
Men turn down the light and burrow
Like moles in the ground;
Only bully, bore and busybody
In beetle-armour clad
Scuttle round and hurry round
With hearts that are glad

18

Has no man the courage to forbid it,
Now that the hounds are so near;
Has all the world no man to rid it
Of the hearts that have caused this fear,
Of the icy hearts and the bragging voices,
So that all the world rejoices
In a day when death was dear?

December 1939

3   *Fool's Song—*1

YESTERDAY is my To-morrow!
  Private joy and private sorrow
Fade out of sight;
(Light, light, more light!)

The grin of the skull
Is now void and null,
Leaving no laughter
To float after.

(Echo cries '"skull" . . . "dull, dull",
Of fools is the world full,
Leaving hereafter
Matter for slaughter!')

Did you see—I saw—a tear
Falling, falling from King Lear,
No moisture giving,
Dry and perfect pearl of steel?

It fell, I tell you, to assuage
The nations that rage,

Mad as he, in wracking fear.
Do *you* think him mad, old Lear,

Because his eyes should thus sweat steel,
Icy, hard and without feel,
That, falling, whizzing, polished round
Can dig his own deep grave in ground?

.   .   .   .

Hollow, my love, hollow your eye
And fie for your bony thigh, fie!
Let me count yours—I'm alive!—
Fingers, one, two, three, four, five!

Let me thank you, as I trace
All your elegance and grace,
Let me thank you for your smile
That will last so long a while.

1941

4   *Fool's Song*—II

THE Emperor Nero
  Falls back to zero

With so much to learn
Of how to bruise and burn.

Why did he waste time on feasts
And singing, when there were the beasts

To watch, let from their fœtid den
To maul and tear the flesh of men?

1941

Journalist's Song

WHO will buy my pretty wares,
   Weeds and tares
Prospering on blood alone
And the marrow of the bone,

All tricked out with pretty favours,
Heigh-ho, Heigh-ho!
Words, according to their flavours,
Heigh-ho, Heigh-ho?

Seductive words for which men die
Every day more willingly,
'Liberty', 'Democracy',
And—foul fiend!—'Autocracy',

Till the whole world to battle goes,
Even butchers pale at the blood that flows,
And the cries of contending hosts
Convert their masters into ghosts.

.   .   .   .   .   .

Come, buy my wares,
Inflate those toy balloons,
Assemble the sacred herds
To their various tunes.

(Do you hear again the summoning bell
That sounds like a falling knife?),
You can change the words I sell
For light or limb or life.

Buy, buy my wares, and trace
How each word can take its toll!
Buy, come buy!   A candle place
For the Emperor Nero's soul!

BEFORE the last few individuals
Are staked upon the ant-heaps
For the dear little creatures to devour,
Let me recapitulate;

I hate high deeds
Mid high, aspiring words,
The bellow of old, blowsy buffaloes.
I love the beauty of the flowering meads
And sun-baked shepherds piping to their herds,
And waters lapping old walls, gold and rose.

I hate the clamorous voices of the crowd,
Its call for all to sacrifice for ever,
Abhor the dronings of its limpet leaders.
I love the quiet talk of those endowed
With reason—call it treason—; the endeavour
To live and love. I hate the million readers

(I love their money, but shall see it never).
I love the panther on its stealthy paws
Leaping from past to future in streaked flash.
I love to prick the bubbles, and to sever
The laws that clutter up effect with cause,
To trip the clown and then to see him crash.

I love the peasant's earth-old cunning,
The look of all things bred from a long line,
And talk up in the air, upon the ladders.
I hate the boasting first, and then the running,
The blatant brag and then regretful whine,
The bloated money-bags that burst like bladders.

I hate war's busy beetles all arrayed
In dung-bright armour of old truth outworn.
I hate the clicking tongues within accustomed grooves,
I love speech to be bitter as a blade,
The unicorn with his rare ivory horn
And centaurs charging crowds with thundering hooves.

7 *Life-Song*

Love of my life, my heart,
Where are we going?
Into what hooded dark
Is yon wind blowing?

'Love of my life', I sang,
'Whence did you roam;
What most elegant and lovely mansion
Did you call your home?'

(. . . 'Oh, how our footfalls die,
Alone, along the darkness burning!
Can we not turn and fly?'
'No.   Time has no turning.')

'Prospered your skin and eye
Under what sky so fair;
What fervent golden wind
Trellised your hair?'

(One and all, are we blown,
Each time our hearts beat,
Further adown this road,
Together always, yet alone.)

'Love that is born in spring
Never can die. . . . Oh!'
So gaudy flowers sing,
Forgetting their shroud, the snow.

> (Watch how the flowers blow,
> Shudder and shiver. . . . Hark!
> Where are our footsteps now?)

We are as beasts at play,
Save that we feel the sting:
Know we know not the way.

> Out of the dark we came,
> And into darkness go:
> Leave me this only flame
> To light my way, my woe!

> Love of my life, my heart,
> Where are we going?
> Into what hooded dark
> Is the wind blowing?

Whence comes the crooked wind
    To set your steeple, witch's hat, a-turning;
Whence comes the light, that rind
    Of fire, to set each stone a-burning;
From what strange mountain in the whiteness lone
Of moon-range comes that wind's quiet moan?

Why is the slanting turret bare,
    Why grow the weeds so rank;
Why are sly windows peeping there,
    And the shadows so lank?
Whence comes your height, seeming higher than your
    neighbour,
Whence comes your wraith-like whiteness in the moon's
    white labour?

Crouching, a shadow lingers, bat–wing'd, at your door,
    Looking down first at the herbs and then up at the stars.
Arching its back, a black cat scampers over the floor,
    In the dark chamber where blossom the stars between
    bars.

Ancient, I ask you, is it the stars you cull
    When you're in darkness, as here with the lank herbs
    below;
Where is the Archer to-night, and the Twins and the Bull?
    Why are the great tides sweeping us to and fro?

On the coast of Coromandel
Dance they to the tunes of Handel;
Chorally, that coral coast
Correlates the bone to ghost,
Till word and limb and note seem one,
Blending, binding act to tone.

All day long they point the sandal
On the coast of Coromandel.
Lemon-yellow legs all bare
Pirouette to peruqued air
From the first green shoots of morn,
Cool as northern hunting horn,
Till the nightly tropic wind
With its rough-tongued, grating rind
Shatters the frail spires of spice.
Imaged in the lawns of rice
(Mirror-flat and mirror-green
Is that lovely water's sheen)
Saraband and rigadoon
Dance they through the purring noon,
While the lacquered waves expand
Golden dragons on the sand—
Dragons that must steaming die
Of the hot sun's agony.

10   *Three Mexican Pieces*

I. DUSK

Night like a hawk
Swooped down
Onto the phoenix bird,

—Tore out its flaming feathers.
Solitary plumes
Flared, falling through darkness,
Floating above the distant sea.
Stillness and heat clung together
And the hawk
Spread out her wings.

Gigantic pinions
Flutter the air above,
Fanning our faces
And
We sing . . .

1919

2. SONG

Ah! Que bonitos
Son los enanos,
Los chiquititos.
Y Mezicanos.
            Old Mexican Song.

How jolly are the dwarfs, the little ones, the Mexicans,
Hidden by the singing of wind through sugar-cane!
Out comes the pretty one,
Out comes the ugly one,
Out comes the dwarf with the wicked smile and thin.

The little women caper and simper and flutter fans,
The little men laugh, stamp, strut and stamp again,
Dance to the bag-pipe drone,
Of insect semitone,
Swelling from ground slashed with light like zebra skin.

The little Cardinal, the humming-bird, whose feathers flare
Like flame across the valley of volcanic stone,

27

Fiery arrow from a rainbow
That the armoured plants have slain, low
Stoops to watch the dwarfs as they dance out of sight.

Hair, long and black as jet, is floating yet on amber air
Honey-shaded by the shadow of Popocatepetl's cone,
Their fluttering *reboses*
Like purple-petal'd roses
Fall through tropic din with a clatter of light.

The crooked dwarf now ripples the strings of a mandoline,
His floating voice has wings that brush us like a butterfly;
Music fills the mountains
With a riot of fountains
That spray back on the hot plain like a waterfall.

Smaller grow the dwarfs, singing 'I'll bring shoes of satin',
Smaller they grow, fade to golden motes, then die.
Where is the pretty one,
Where is the ugly one,
Where is that tongue of flame, the little Cardinal?

1919

3. MAXIXE

Los enanitos
Se enajaren.
Old Mexican Song.

THE Mexican dwarfs can dance for miles
Stamping their feet and scattering smiles,
Till the loud hills laugh and laugh again
At the dancing dwarfs in the golden plain,
Till the bamboos sing as the dwarfs dance by,
Kicking their feet at a jagged sky,
That torn by leaves and gashed by hills
Rocks to the rhythm the hot sun shrills;

The bubble sun stretches shadows that pass
To noiseless jumping-jacks of glass,
So long and thin, so silent and opaque,
That the lions shake their orange manes, and quake;
And a shadow that leaps over Popocatepetl
Terrifies the tigers as they settle
Cat-like limbs, cut with golden bars,
Under bowers of flowers that shimmer like stars.
Buzzing of insects flutters above,
Shaking the rich trees' treasure-trove
Till the fruit rushes down like a comet, whose tail
Thrashes the night with its golden flail,
The fruit hisses down with a plump from its tree
Like the singing of a rainbow as it dips into the sea.
The loud red trumpets of great blossoms blare
Triumphantly like heralds who blow a fanfare,
Till the humming-bird, bearing heaven on its wing,
Flies from the terrible blossoming,
And the humble honey-bee is frightened by the fine
Honey that is heavy like money and purple like wine,
While birds that flaunt their pinions like pennons
Shriek from their trees of oranges and lemons,
And the scent rises up in a cloud, to make
The swinging, hairy monkeys feel so weak
That they each throw down a bitten coconut or mango.

.   .   .   .

Up flames a flamingo, over the fandango.
Glowing like a fire and gleaming like a ruby,
From Guadalajara to Guadalupe
It flies—in flying drops a feather,
—And the snatching dwarfs stop dancing, to fight together.
1919

I. CORNUCOPIA

Now music fills the night with moving shades;
Its velvet darkness, veinèd like a grape,
Obscures and falls round many a subtle shape
—Figures that steal through cool, tall colonnades,
Vast minotaurian corridors of sleep;
Rhythmic they pass us, splashed by red cascades
Of wine; fierce-flashing fountains, whose proud waves
Shimmer awhile, plunge foaming over steep
Age-polished rocks into the dim, cold caves
Of starlit dusk below—then merge in night

But yet more figures sway into our sight;
Strong and bare-shouldered, pressed and laden down,
Stagger across the terraces.   They bear
Great cornucopia of summer fruit
And heavy roses scented with the noon
—Piled up with fruit and blossom, all full-blown,
Crimson, or golden as the harvest moon—
Piled up and overflowing in a flood
Of riches; brilliant-plumaged birds, that sing
With the faint playing of a far, sweet lute,
Warble their tales of conquest and of love;
Perch on each shoulder; sweep each rainbow wing
Like lightning through the breathless dark above.
Heaped up in vases, gems shine hard and bright;
Sudden they flare out—gleaming red like blood—
For now the darkness turns to ragged light;
Great torches gild each shadow, tear the sky,
As drums tear through the silence of the night,
Breaking its crystal quiet—making us cry
Or catch our sobbing breath in sudden fear.

A shadow stumbles, and the jewels shower
On to the pavers, in a sharp rebound
To mingle with the fountain drops that flower
Up in a scarlet bloom above the ground,
A beauteous changing blossom; then they rain
On to the broad, mysterious terraces,
Where Sea-Gods rise to watch in cold disdain
Before those vast vermilion palaces,
—Watch where the slumbering coral gods of noon,
Drunk with the sudden golden light and flare
Of flaming torches, try to pluck and tear
That wan enchanted lotus flower, the moon,
Down from its calm still waters;

                         Thus they fall,
Like flowing plumes, the fountains of our festival.

. . . .

Slowly the torches die.   They echo long,
These last notes of a Bacchanalian song,
Of drifting, drowsy beauty, born of sleep,
—Vast as the sea, as changing and as deep.
In thanksgiving for shelt'ring summer skies
Still, far away, a fervent red flame glows.
Small winds brush past against our lips and eyes,
Caress them like a laughing summer rose,
And rainbow moths flit by, in circling flight.
A harp sobs out its crystal syrupings;
Faintly it sounds, as the bright chequer'd wings,
Fragile yet radiant, of a butterfly
Beating against the barriers of night.

Then from the Ocean came the Siren song,
With perfume heavy, yet soft as a sigh,

Kissing our minds, and changing right from wrong;
Chaining our limbs; making our bodies seem
Inert and spellbound, dead as in a dream.

1918

2. SONG

Our hidden voices, wreathèd with love's flowers,
Wind-toss'd through valleys, tremble across seas
To turban'd cities; touch tall, lonely towers,
Call to you through the sky, the wind, the trees.

Misted and golden as the hanging moon,
That like a summer fruit floats from the sky,
Thrills out our distant, age-enchanted tune,
—Nor will it let you pass our beauty by.
But if it should not reach to stir your mind,
Then hold a summer rose against the ear,
Till through its crimson sweetness you can hear
The falling flow of rhythm—so design'd
That from this secret island, like a star
Shining above a shrouded world, our song
Cleaves through the darkest night and echoes long,
Bidding you follow, whether near or far,
Come hither where the mermaids churn the foam,
Lashing their tails across the calm, or dive
To groves and gardens of bright flowers, then roam
Beneath the shadow of stone trees, or drive
Some slow sea-monster to its musselled home.
Here, as a ladder, they climb up and down
The rainbow's steep, refracted steps of light,
Till, when the dusk sends down its rippling frown,
They quiver back to us in silver flight.
The moon sails up once more; our mermaids bring
Rich gifts of ocean fruit.   Again we sing.

Enchantment, love, vague fear, and memories
That cling about us like the fumes of wine,
With myriad love-enhancing mysteries
We pour out in one song—intense—divine,
Down the deep, moonlit chasm of the waves
Our song floats on the opiate breeze.   Why seek
To goad your carven galley, fast-bound slaves
Who search each sweeping line of bay and creek,
Only to stagger on a rock, or find
The limp, dead sails swept off by sudden wind?
Thus always you must search the cruel sea,
For if you find us, mankind shall be free!

But when you sleep we grasp you by the hand,
And to the trickling honey of the lute
We lead you to a distant, shimmering land
Where lotus-eaters munch their golden fruit,
Then fall upon the fields of summer flowers
In drunken sunlit slumber, while a fawn
Prances and dances round them.

                                        Oh, those hours,
When through the crystal valleys of the dawn
Down from the haunted forests of the night
There dash the dew-drenched centaurs on their way,
Mad with the sudden rush of golden light
—Affright the lotus-eaters, as they sway
Toward the woodland in a stumbling flight.
In those deep groves we follow through the cool
Shadow of high, columnar trees, to find
The fallen sky within a forest pool
Now faintly veiled and fretted by a wind,
Lest our white-flashing limbs should turn you blind.

1918

33   c

WHEN SOLOMON MET THE QUEEN OF SHEBA

*'And she gave the king an hundred and twenty talents of gold, and
of spices very great store, and precious stones . . .
    And the navy also of Hiram, that brought gold from Ophir, brought
in from Ophir great plenty of almug* trees, and precious stones.'*
1 KINGS X.

THE navy at Ezion-Geba
    Gazed across the water amazed
When Solomon met the Queen of Sheba;
E'en lions in the desert were dazed
With wonder at her striped pavilion
That blazed like a new parhelion.
They roared their admiration
At this strange coruscation
            Till the satyrs
                Took their tawny children
                    Trampling through the sand
To march with the procession, to march with the band.
The flaming phoenix flew with its feathers to fan
The Queen at the head of her caravan;
But, the phoenix, though famously fabulous,
Was jealous, envious, and emulous,
            For the Queen of Sheba had a retinue
            Strictly in keeping with her revenue—
Six thousand camels and camelopards,
Ten thousand and ninety nigger bodyguards.
The camelopards, stiff-necked and tall,
Would scarce deign to notice the Queen at all,
But the proud though kindly camels kneel,
Offer their humps for the Queen to feel,

* '*algum*, n. Tree mentioned in Bible (2 Chron. ii. 8; in 1 Kings x. 11
wrongly given as *almug*), prob. a kind of sandal-wood [Heb.; a foreign word
perh. = Skr. *valguka* sandal-wood tree].'—The Concise Oxford Dictionary.

Nodding arched necks and plumes of ostrich-feather,
Dyed like her bright Abyssinian weather,
While ten thousand niggers beat on gourds and golden gongs,
Slashing the air with their piebald songs,

.   .   .   .

Thus the Queen met the King at Jerusalem,
And he
      Seemed wiser
              Than Methuselem:
With a great black beard,
            And a nose like a scythe,
He lived in the palace,
             And subsisted on a tithe!
   He gave the Queen of Sheba a welcome
   Proportionate to her income;
But this amazing Amazon
Was lovable, generous and free,
She brought a gift to Solomon of cinnamon,
With an Almug and a Nutmeg tree.
     These he placed before his palace
     For the pleasant
           Stupefaction
                Of the populace.
Each sweet-smelling branch bore a budding bell of gold
(Oh! the blood of the Israelites ran cold . . .),
When evening-wind blurred the hills with blue
The swinging and the singing of the bells sang true
These by some magic stratagem
Played the Sheban National Anthem,
While the trill of each bell was like an Abyssinian bird,
Or the golden voice of the Queen—for each word
She spoke, trembled, sparkled in the air,
Then spread its wings, and flew from her.

But the Queen of Sheba went with Solomon
　　　　To his country house at Lebanon,
Where she brought him gifts of hot-house grapes,
Of ivory,
　　　　Of ebony,
　　　　　　　Of elephants and apes,
Of peacocks, of pearls, and a hundred pygmy slaves
With skins like an orange, and hair that waves.
Above it, each wore a turban,
Picked out with the plumes of a pelican—
But of all her gifts, by far the rarest,
Brought from the terrible central forest,
With a vein of gold in its ivory horn,
Was a lovelorn
　　　　Milk-white
　　　　　　Unicorn.
　　　But the King, though sweet as honey,
　　　Had an eye for the value of money,
So he only gave her an heraldic lion
Embossed with the arms (and nose) of Zion.

　　·　　·　　·　　·　　·　　·　　·　　·　　·　　·

　　Though the Queen of Sheba loved Solomon
　　She was not happy at Lebanon:
It was not the women of the Edomites,
The Zidonians,
　　　　The Moabites,
　　　　　　The Hittites,
　　　　　　　Or the Ammonites!
She would even listen to his Proverbs, she put up with very
　　　　many wrongs—
But in secretly reading his notebook, she found Solomon's
　　　　'Song-of-Songs.'

She knew it at once—it was poetry! . . . And she left the
  palace that day,
But Solomon knew not where she went to nor why she had
  roamed away!
      But every evening in Jerusalem
      The Almug and the Nutmeg trees
      Flaunt the Sheban National Anthem
      Like a banner on the spice-laden breeze.
(And oh! each golden bell
      Seemed a turtle-dove
            That coo'd
Within the moonlight shadow
      Of an Abyssinian wood.) . . .

. . . .

But we wonder what she looked like—this phantom or
  phantasmagoria,
Atalanta, Gioconda, Semiramis—or the late Queen Victoria?

13   *Two Garden Pieces and Parade*

I. FOUNTAIN

PROUD fountain, wave your plumes,
  Spread out your phoenix-wing,
Let the tired trees rejoice
Beneath your blossoming
(Tired trees, you whisper low)

High up, high up, above
These green and drooping sails,
A fluttering young wind
Hovers and dives—but fails
To steal a foaming feather.

37

Sail, like a crystal ship,
Above your sea of glass;
Then, with your quickening touch,
Transmute the things that pass
(Come down, cool wind, come down).

All humble things proclaim,
Within your magic net,
Their kinship to the Gods.
More strange and lovely yet
All lovely things become.

Dead sculptured stones assume
The life from which they came;
The kingfisher is now
A moving tongue of flame,
A blue, live tongue of flame,

While birds, less proud of wing,
Crouch, in wind-ruffled shade,
Hide shyly, then pour out,
Their jealous serenade;
(Close now your golden wings!)

2. NEPTUNE IN CHAINS

Enslaved are the old Gods;
Pan pipes soundlessly
For the unheeding bees.

Bound by the trailing tresses of the vine
To soft captivity,
Neptune has left his waves
To stand beneath the frozen, green cascades
Of summer trees.

Is the Sea-God, then, content to rule
The rippling of wayward flowers,
Lulled by the songs that many birds pour out
From their green cradles, gently-rocked
—Songs that foam like hissing rain
Among the heavy blossoms?
Can he control
The music of the wind through poplar trees,
—Those trees, an instrument
That any wind, however young
Or drunk with drowsing scent
Of petals, crushed by the flaming fingers of the sun,
Can play upon?

But darkness the deliverer
Comes with dreams.
Night's grape-stained waves
Cool his aching body—
The song of the nightingale
Falls round him
Like the froth of little waves;
The warm touch of the evening wind
Thaws the green cascades
Till you can hear
Every liquid sound within the world,
Fountains, falling waterfalls
And the low murmur of the rolling sea
—And Neptune dreams that he is free.

3. PARADE

WHILE vapour rises, the sun shines along
A promenade beneath tall trees.   In vain
Seek thirsting flowers to thread their crystal song
Upon the liquid harpstrings of the rain.

Sweet air is honey'd with the lulling sound
Of bees, gold-dusted. In the avenue
Each leaf is now a lens the sun has found
To focus light, and cast green shadow through

Where walks Zenobia. Her marmoset
Perched on the shoulder, grabs at ribbon'd flowers
Or youthful curls of elders. Etiquette
Is outraged, and a dowager glowers.

The marmoset attacks Zenobia's curls,
Clutches the papillon's enamel'd sail;
Gesticulates with idiot hands; unfurls,
Then counts, the piebald rings upon his tail.

Here flutter fan and feather to and fro
As eager birds caressing golden sheaves;
And like the spray of fountains when winds blow,
The froth of laughter foams among the leaves,

Till music, thin as silver wire, uncoils
—Metallic trap to trip unwary players—
A tune, ringed like the monkey's tail; but foils
Any attempt to straighten it. In layers

The idlers form, to watch the stage, where leap
These masked buffoons to which the Old Gods sank.
Over her fan Zenobia may peep
At the lewd gestures of a mountebank.

The silent lime-trees drip their golden scent;
Staccato shrills the puppet, waves a wand,
Postures, exaggerates a sentiment. . . .
The little ape, alone, may understand

How men make Gods, and place them high above;
Then clamber up themselves to throw God down.
Dearly pay deities for former love:
We hold them captive, make them play the clown.

Who knows but that one day men may be bound
Thus to make war or love for apish laughter,
Until the world of gibbering monkeys round
Quiver with laughter at our simian slaughter?

.   .   .   .

End song and antic; players quit the stage
To the gloved silence of genteel applause,
Splutters El Capitan in Spanish rage,
Curses his money.   Swathed in quiet, like gauze,

The earth is still, until a breeze sets free
Green leaves, with plucking sound of mandoline.
Convulsed the monkey capers—seems to see
The wind, that wingèd God and Harlequin,

Who, flying down, sounds waters' silver strings
And brings soft music from far trembling towers,
Snatches a bird-bright feather for his wings
And flickers light on many secret flowers

14   *Nocturne*

THE valleys that we knew in sunlit hours
   Are vast and vague as seas,
Wan as the blackthorn flowers
That quiver in the first spring-scented breeze;
Far as the frosted hollows of the moon.

The sighing woods are still
That climb this mouse-soft hill,
Tall nettles rank with rain
Scent all the woods with some ancestral fear.

Trees rustle by the water—Soon
A voice sings near,
Too loud, to ward off fright:
Then fainter, and in vain,
Sings in the yielding and unechoing night.

15   *Lausiac Theme*

SERAPION-THE-SINDONITE
Wore a cloth about his loins.
This Christian Recondite
Never carried coins:

Never did he ask for bread;
Revelled in his own distress,
High of spirit, low of head.
With no other dress

Than a cloth, Serapion
Was free from greed and gluttony;
Progressed in the direction
Of impassivity.

Serapion, though ascetic,
Could not keep within his cell—
Spiritual athletic,
Who wrestled with Hell:

This Sindonitic holy man
Converted, overcome by pity,
Thaïs, the famous courtesan,
To Christianity.

Thaïs was not thin or frail,
But full of figure.   Flesh and blood
Rose up in riot—made her rail
At a selfless God.

From Theban windows, far above,
She plays and sings to a guitar
With low voice: the light of love
Beckons like a star.

Eagerly she welcomed in
The unexpected Sindonite;
But he spoke to her of sin—
Set her soul alight.

So they went together out
To the crowded, garish street,
Where he taught her how to flout
Fumes of wine and meat.

To the Thebaid they go—
Where she stands each Christian test,
Plaiting palm-leaves to and fro,
Sure of heaven's rest.

In the desert they both died,
Thaïs and the holy man.
They were buried side by side,
Ascetic and courtesan.

To Margaret Greville

I

Now night,
                    The sighing night,
Descends to hide and heal
The crimson wounds
Ripped in the sky
Where the high helmet-towers
(With clouds as streaming feathers)
Have torn the heavens
In their incessant sunset battle.
Below,
        Upon the mound,
Small golden flowers
Release their daylight slowly
At the Night's behest,
Till they become pale discs
That quiver
When the evening wind
Draws his thin fingers
Down the dew-drenched grass
—As an old harper,
Who awakes
From drunken sunlit slumber,
Blindly plucks
His silver-sounding strings—
Making the sound
That, further, darker down
The trees make,
When they draw back
Their upturned leaves
In fountain-foaming hurry.

The curling, hump-backed dolphins,
Drunk with purple fumes
Of wine-stained sunset,
Plunge through the wider waters of the night—
Waters that well down every narrow street
In darkening billows,
Till they become quiet, full—
Canals that, mirror-like,
Reflect each sound
Of snarling song
In all the town.

And, as the dolphins dive,
There splashes back
Upon their goat-eared riders,
Dislodged in sudden fury,
The foaming froth of summer-cooling winds
—Issuing from where the northern trees
Bellow their resined breath
Across the seas
To ripple through far fields
Of twilight flowers—
Sweeping across
To where these old high towers
Of Carcassonne
Still stand to break their flow.

Neptune, from his high pedestal,
Can watch the waters of the night
Rise, further, further,
And the faun-riders sink below
The conquering, cool tide.

I

From my high window,
From my high window in a Southern city,
I peep through the slits of the shutters,
Whose steps of light
Span darkness like a ladder.
Throwing wide the shutters
I let the streets into the silent room
With sudden clatter;
Walk out upon the balcony
Whose curving irons are bent
Like bows about to shoot—
Bows from which the mortal arrows
Cast from dark eyes, dark-lashed
And shadowed by mantillas,
Shall in the evening
Rain down upon men's hearts
Paraded here, in southern climes,
More openly,
But, at this early moment of the day,
The balconies are empty;
Only the sun, still drowsy-fingered,
Plucks, *pizzicato*, at the rails,
Draws out of them faint music
Of rain-washed air,
Or, when each bell lolls out its idiot tongue,
When Time lets drop his cruel scythe,
They sing in sympathy
The sun, then, plucks these irons,
As far below,
That child
Draws his stick along the railings.

46

The sound of it brings my eye down to him. . . .
Oh heart, dry heart,
It is yourself again.
How nearly are we come together!
If, at this moment,
One long ribbon was unfurled
From me to him,
I should be shown
Above, in a straight line—
A logical growth,
And yet,
    I wave, but he will not look up;
    I call, but he will not answer.

2

From where I stand
The beauty of the early morning
Suffocates me;
It is as if fingers closed round my heart.
The light flows down the hills in rivulets,
So you could gather it up in the cup of your hands,
While pools,
The cold eyes of the gods,
Are cradled in those hollows.
Cool are the clouds,
Anchored in the heaven;
Green as ice are they,
To temper the heat in the valleys
With arches of violet shadow.
You can hear from the distant woods
The thud of the centaurs' hoofs
As they gallop down to drink,
Shatter the golden roofs

47

Of the trees, for swift as the wind
They gallop down to the brink
Of the waters that echo their laughter,
Cavernous as rolling of boulders down hills;
Lolling, they lap at the gurgling waters.

.　　.　　.　　.　　.　　.　　.

But nearer rises the sound,
Red, ragged as his comb,
Of a cock crowing;
A bird flies up to me at the window,
Leaping, like music, with regular rhythm,
Sinks down, then, to the city beneath.

3

Dressed, here, in bright colours,
The ants below are hurrying down the footways.
Under their various intolerable burdens
They stagger along.
Stop to converse, move, wave their antennæ.

.　　.　　.　　.　　.　　.　　.

The fruit-seller is opening his stall,
Oranges are piled in minute pyramids,
While melons, green melons,
Swing from the roof in string cradles.
The butcher festoons his shop
With swags and gay wreaths of entrails;
Beautiful heads with horns,
Are nailed up, as on pagan altars,
(Though their ears are fresh from the hearing
Of Orpheus playing his lute).

The Aguador arranges his glasses,
Out of which the sun will strike
His varying scales of crystal music
This afternoon, round the arena.
The Matador prepares for the fight,
Is, indeed, already in the tavern,
Where later and refreshed with blood,
He will celebrate his triumph
Among the poignant kindling
Of strìngèd instruments.

. . . .

—But the child has run away crying;
I call—but no answer comes.

4

The chatter of the daylight grows
As I look upon the market-place,
Where there is a droning of bag-pipes,
And the hard, wooden music of the hills;
The housewife has left her cottage in the forest,
Driving here through the early tracks of the sun.
The beggars are already at their posts,
Their dry flesh peeps through their garments.
Their old ritual whining
Causes no show of pity.
Why should the hucksters, the busy people notice?
God himself has stood here, out at elbows,
Waiting patiently in the market-place,
While they chatter in gay booths
But how I fear for them,
These who are not afraid!
I shout to them to make them understand.

They talk more, cease talking and look up,
They all look up, remain gaping.

.   .   .   .

I went back into the water-cool room,
Put on my coloured coat, my buskin,
And mask of Harlequin.
They see me, this time.
'Come on, come on,' they cry,
'You are just in time.
There is fun down here in the market-place.
Two men have been run over,
And there's to be a public execution.
The gallows are nearly up
—And after, in the evening,
We will go round the wineshops,
Strumming guitars,
While trills Dolores in her wide, red skirt.
Oh come on, come on!'
—But the paint from my mask runs down
And dyes my clothing.

5

It is not thus in the Northern cities,
Where the cold breathes close to the window-pane,
Where the brittle flowers of the frost
Crackle at the window's edge.
From my window in the Northern city
I can hear the rattle and roar of the town,
As the carts go lumbering over the bridges,
As the men in dark clothes hurry over the bridges.
They do not parade their hearts here,
They bury them at their lives' beginning.
They must hurry, or they will be late for their work;
Their work is their bread.

Without bread, how can they work?
They have no time for pleasure,
Nor is work any pleasure to them.
Their faces are masked with weariness,
Drab with their working.
(Only the tramp who moves among them
Unnoticed, despised,
Has eyes that have seen)
They must work till the guns go again,
Giving them their only pretence to glory.
They have no time to fear,
No time to think of an end.
Foolishly I called to them on the bridges;
Only a few stopped, looked up
—But these were convulsed with fury.
Said one to another
'I have never seen a man
Behave like that before.'
But most of them were mute;
They could not see.

. . . .

Through the murkiness of the Northern dawn,
The gas already flares out
In the glass palaces
Where to-night, weary and dulled with smoke and with
    drink,
They will seek, in a brief oblivion,
Laughter, and the mask of Ally Sloper.

. . . . . .

Thus it is in the Northern cities,
Where the cold lies close to the window-pane,
Where the grass grows its little blades of steel
And the wind is armed with seven whips.

6

Happy is Orpheus as he plays,
The dumb beasts listen quietly,
The music strokes their downy ears,
Melts the fierce fire within them.

Only with music can you tame the beasts,
Break them of their grizzly feasts;
Only with music can you open eyes to wonder.

. . . .

But if they will not hear?
The people have lost faith in music,
Few are there to call, and none to answer.

. . . .

When the Prince kissed the Sleeping Beauty,
He broke the wicked spell of cobwebs;
She answered, opened her eyes.

When Narcissus looked into the pool,
The cruel waters gave him their reply:
Even that was a better fate
Than to cry out in the lonely night
—And not to be answered.

7

From my high window in a Southern city,
One can see beyond the geometrical array
Of roofs, of Roman camps, now squares,
And intersecting streets,
Into far valleys;
Blue open flowers
Cupped between mountains.

The forests are so far away
They creep like humble green moss
Over mounds that are mountains.
But there, mid the deep penetrating glow
Of sunlight piercing through green leaves,
Sounds other music than the falling streams

8

When Orpheus with his wind-swift fingers
Ripples the strings that gleam like rain,
The wheeling birds fly up and sing,
Hither, thither, echoing
There is a crackling of dry twigs,
A sweeping of leaves along the ground.
Tawny faces and dumb eyes
Peer through unfluttering green screens
That mask ferocious teeth and claws,
Now tranquil.
As the music sighs upon the hills,
The young
Come skipping, ambling, rolling down,
Their soft ears flapping as they run,
Their fleecy coats catching in the thickets,
Till they lie, listening, round his feet.

. . . .

Unseen for centuries,
Fabulous creatures creep out of their caverns.
The Unicorn
Prances down from his bed of leaves,
His milk-white muzzle still stainèd green
With the munching, crunching of mountain herbs
The Griffin usually so fierce,
Now tame and amiable again—

Has covered the bones in his secret cavern
With a rustling pall of dank, dead leaves,
While the Salamander—true lover of art—
Flickers, then creeps out of the flame;
Gently now, and away he goes,
Kindles his proud and blazing track
Across the forest,
Drawn to this melodious glade
Where, listening, he may cool his fever.

.   .   .   .

When the housewife returns,
Carrying her basket,
She will not understand.
She misses nothing,
Has heard nothing in the woods.
She will only see
That the fire is dead,
The grate cold.

.   .   .   .

But the child left in the empty house
Saw the Salamander leave the flame,
Heard a strange wind, like music, in the forest,
And has gone out to look for it,
Alone.

Winter the Huntsman

I. THE SWORD AND THE HERB

THE double-crowned king
      Sleeps in his tomb,
For deep in his pyramid
The sword and the herb are laid.

The herb is the incense,
The sword is the flame,
The King is the Hierarch,
Darkness or dust the same.

To guard him from these
Two quilting enemies,
Stand the sharp angle of the pyramid
And pathetic art of the embalmer.

.   .   .   .   .   .

The double-crowned king
Sleeps in his tomb,
By him in the darkness muffled
Sharp sword and sweet herb are laid.

2. NEW MAGIC

THE witches are gone,
  Their broomsticks are broken,
The owl flies forlorn
  Now that no spell is spoken.

The Triple Tiara,
  Confined to a tower,
Like Abra-Cadabra
  Has lost its old power,

And no more the cauldrons bubble
  On any blasted heath,
No more the bent hags babble,
  Gabble their spells and mumble death,

For the incense that rises
　　Is smoke from a factory.
Though Man now despises
　　All flames expiatory,

Yet vast furnaces cast
　　Spells, blacker by far
Than those of the past,
　　With their 'per cent' and 'par,'

And the new race of sombre Man and sullen
　　Moans in its sleep and turns,
No trust in Hell or Heaven,
　　In fixed star that shines or deep fire that burns.

Yes, the witches are gone,
　　Their broomsticks are broken,
The owl flies forlorn
　　Now that no spell is spoken!

3. 'THEN ARE THE WOODS SO EMPTY?'

'THEN are the woods so empty
That used to be so full,
Does no hidden life stir in them,
Is there no storm and sudden lull?

'Does no leaf tremble without reason,
Like the breathing of a man who hides?
Is there never now a running tremor
Under those green and morose tides,

'Where, frosted with heavy dew,
Drenched, lies the summer grass
Over which the moon-shadows
Palely pass and repass,

56

'Where, tall as the creaking trees,
The chalk-white shadows stalk
Till another sudden breeze
Whips them back to the dark?

.   .   .   .   .   .

'Does no leaf tremble without reason,
Like the breathing of a man who hides?
Is there never now a wind-swift ripple
Through those billowing blue tides?'

4. '. . . WHEN THE OWL AT NIGHT'

'PERHAPS . . . When the owl at night
Deep in the moon-washed wood
For her own delight
Teaches her hornèd brood

'To fall from a branch,
With a flutter-flapping wing,
And moan like a ghost
Round the empty ring,

'Where once purred the flames
Of her ancient allies
That, like cats, arched and hissed,
Flashing their baleful eyes . . .

'Perhaps then one believes
That the woods are yet full
And a meaning still lurks
In sudden storm or lull,

'That the witch still waits
Her time to return,
And somewhere hidden
The old fires burn,

'That the broomstick, broken
Will bud again from the fertile earth;
And the double-crowned King be woken
To a new and more painful birth.'

5. SUPERSTITION . . .

YES . . . The witches are gone,
Their broomsticks are broken,
The owl hoots forlorn
Now that no spell is spoken.

. . . .

But, looking for eglantine,
Columbine, celandine,
Wolfsbane and oxbane,
Sainfoin and fluellin,
Wortdragon, snapdragon,
Martagon, campion,
Tarragon, rampion,
Rocambole, pompion,
Deborah, under her wide black hat,
In her dress of beetle's wing,
Wanders through the meadows
That are full of nodding and sighing,
    Sighing and nodding,
Where, swinging on their slender stems,
The bell-flowers ring their curfew gentle
For the old woman under her wide black hat,
In her green-black mantle.

. . . .

She must wait till the last gold turns to silver,
Till the moon throws off his steel cuirass
Of cloud, and all the tall trees shiver
At water and light divisionless.

Then through marine groves slowly brushes
Old Deborah the herbalist,
To pick a thousand verdigris grasses
—The evening dew her alchemist—,
Looking for eglantine,
Columbine, celandine,
Wolfsbane and oxbane,
Sainfoin and fluellin,
Wortdragon, snapdragon,
Martagon, campion,
Tarragon, rampion,
Rocambole, pompion.

6. AND SCIENCE

SHE can see from her grove
The far tongues of the furnaces,
Where the huge red mouths grin
And bellow bull-menaces,

Or with greedy-pleasure gurgle
As they ever munch fresh food,
For the mandibles of those ogres
Dribble day and night with blood.

.   .   .   .   .   .

The herbalist's brewings
Are mere superstition;
She lacks education
And all erudition.

She does not appeal
To the rational brain,
But to dim, antique instincts
Of fear or faith in man.

She could never distil
From a few cabbage-stalks
Enough force to kill
A million men,

While each day and everywhere
Men of science enjoy
The process of finding
New ways to destroy,

Till all round the globe
Complete is the circle,
Of germ in its tube
And shell in its cradle.

.   .   .   .   .   .

The double-crowned king
Rests in his pyramid,
By him for his long winter
Sharp sword and sweet herb are laid.

7. WINTER THE HUNTSMAN

THROUGH his iron glades
Rides Winter the Huntsman.
All colour fades
As his horn is heard sighing.

Far through the forest
His wild hooves crash and thunder
Till many a mighty branch
Is torn asunder

And the red reynard creeps
To his hole near the river,
The copper leaves fall
And the bare trees shiver.

As night creeps from the ground,
Hides each tree from its brother,
And each dying sound
Reveals yet another.

Is it Winter the Huntsman
Who gallops through his iron glades,
Cracking his cruel whip
To the gathering shades?

8. DANSE MACABRE *

THE Countess Klondyke
Was of rather humble origin,
Though her pompadour-peruke
And her smile, as of a cherubin,

Both throw-out a widow-theme
That is Spanish Cosmopolitan
And *Ancien-Régime*
More than Broadway-American.

Her fortune increased
Of itself—an automaton—
Till gold-leaf encased
The family-skeleton,
Which danced
And pranced
Till light from each limb flashed
And bones crashed like castanets,
But, by no threats abashed
And quelled by no epithets,

* To a Spanish dance-tune.

In family-tomb and factory
Is maintained its mad *jota*!
Revealing when refractory
The fact that the Quota
Not so long ago
Was not—
Then, as though now in vertigo,
Proceeded to foot
A reverberant gavotte
—Like the virulent virago
That it was—as a parting shot!

.   .   .   .

Now the Countess Klondyke,
Though modern and materialist,
Entertained a dislike
For this puritan casuist:

So she feigned not to hear the bones
That rattled and dangled,
For the glint of the gold
That sparkled and spangled.

For she did not believe
In things which she did not see
—Therefore if she looked the other way
Those things could not be!

9. OUT IN THE GARDEN

WINTER, wild Huntsman,
Swept through his glassy glades,
Crunching under crackling hooves
Crisp spires and brittle blades

Twisted with flowers of steel,
—Cold, hard petals of crystal
That yet wither at a touch,
So pure are they and vestal.

The quivering lawns
Burn with this alpine fire,
To life fanned in the dawn's
Innermost and most secret spire.

In a glade of the garden
The Triton stands frozen,
His clear song must harden
To music made visible,

While each gurgling note,
By white magic transmuted,
As it leaves his stone throat
Is changed into solid light.

10. THE FLEDGELING

BOUND there by biting thongs,
Triton in vain must blow,
With swollen cheeks, a conch
Where nests a young rainbow;

That rare, that most fabulous bird,
Flaming roc and dripping phoenix,
Whose song is, so seldom heard,
Of green things all growing, growing!

Sun and rain gave it birth,
Swift it swoops down its arc:
A flutter of fiery wings to earth,
A swooping flight as of a hawk.

Then the song hovers and shrills,
Till its feathers dissolve again
Into eyes of light on the hills
And the beating wings of the rain.

II. 'WHICH IS THE TRITON TRUE?'

WHILE the water's smooth canticles
And the verdure's brittle spires
Are transformed into icicles
And quivering fires,

Bound there by biting thongs
Must Triton in vain blow,
With swollen cheeks, the conch
Where nests this young rainbow?

But this—this, shivering from stone hips
Cannot be the Triton true,
Who, double music at redoubled lips,
Shows in two orbs of blue

Each summer—till you wonder
Which is real, this grey stone
Against the peacock-sky, or under,
Where he plunges up through the unruffled pool?

·   ·   ·   ·   ·   ·   ·   ·

Out in the garden
The Triton stands frozen,
His clear song must harden
To music made visible.

But the water beneath
Is now coffined by Winter,
Who hunts to the death
And tears one from the other.

Mute and alone he stands
—Yet at first breath of Spring,
Shall Triton break his bonds
And to his image sing!

12. THE GARDENER

THE lawns are aquiver
With petals of crystal,
That at a touch wither,
So pure are they and vestal,

When the bass-bearded Califf
Leaves his palace, the potting-shed
(Where on each stove-warmed shelf
Recline golden bulbs or red),

To garner the fruit,
To smooth all the trees,
And shelter exotics
From the steel-billed breeze.

The gardener's task,
Indeed, is eternal
To keep Nature tidy
In regions hibernal:

No time for the Triton—
He brushes the path,
Piling dark leaves in mounds,
To meet a fiery death.

When dusk falls again
Black as in a pyramid,
Smoulders the bonfire
Till both flame and herb are dead.

But under the darkness dour
The spires of the grass are yet
Ready to flame once more
At the tread of the dawn's swift feet.

19 *Night*

ALL the dim terrors dwelling far below,
Interr'd by many thousand years of life,
Arise to revel in this evil dark:
The wail forlorn of dogs that mourn for men;
A shuffling footfall on a creaking board;
The handle of a door that shakes and turns;
A door that opens slightly, not enough;
The rustling sigh of silk along a floor;
The knowledge of being watched by one long dead,
By something that is outside Nature's pale;
The unheard sounds that haunt an ancient house;
The feel of one who listens in the dark,
Listens to that which happened long ago,
Or what will happen after we are dust;
The awful waiting for a near event;
Or for a crash to rend the silence deep
Enveloping a house that always waits—
A house that whispers to itself and weeps;
The murmur of the yew, or woodland cries,
A sombre note of music on the breeze;

A shudder from the ivy that entwines
The horror that is felt within its grip;
The sound of prowling things that walk abroad,
The nauseous flapping of Night's bat-like wings;
These are the signs the gods have given us
To know the limit of our days and powers.

The Beginning

GREAT spheres of fire, to which the sun is naught,
Pass thund'ring round our world.   A golden mist—
The margin to the universe—falls round
The verges of our vision.   Rocks ablaze
Leap upward to the sun, or fall beneath
The rush of our rapidity, that seems
Catastrophe, and not the joyous birth
Of yet another star.   The air is full
Of clashing colour, full of sights and sounds
Too plain and loud for men to heed or hear,
The cosmic cries of pain that follow birth:
A multi-coloured world.

                     The scorching heat
Surpasses all the equatorial days:
Steam rises from the surface of the sea.
Gigantic rainbow mists resemble forms
That bring to mind strange elemental sprites
Exulting in the chaos of creation
They glide above the tumult-ridden sea
Which now is shaken as are autumn leaves;
Great hollows open and reveal its depths,
Devoid of any form of life—or death.

Till, wave on wave, it gathers strength again
And shakes a mountain, splits it to the base
(Still weak from struggle as a new-born babe).
Then night comes on, and shows the flaming path
Of all the rocks that vainly seek the sun.

Broad as the arch of space, a myriad moons
Sail slowly by the sea; the glowing world
Sets off the pallor of their ivory.
The din grows greater from the universe:
There rises up the smell of fire and iron—
Not dreary like the smell of burnt-out things,
But like the smell of some gigantic forge—
Cheerful, of good intent, and full of life.

Now all the joyous cries of sea and earth,
The universal harmonies of birth,
Rise up to haunt the slumber of their God.

21 *The End*

Round the great ruins crawl those things of slime;
Green ruins, lichenous and scarred by moss—
An evil lichen that proclaims world doom,
Like blood dried brown upon a dead man's face.
And nothing moves save those monstrosities,
Armoured and grey, and of a monster size.

But now, a thing passed through the cloying air
With flap and clatter of its scaly wings—
As if the whole world echoed from some storm.

One scarce could see it in the dim, green light
Till suddenly it swooped and made a dart
And brushed away one of those things of slime,
Just as a hawk might sweep upon its prey.

It seems as if the light grows dimmer yet—
No radiance from the dreadful green above,
Only a lustrous light or iridescence
As if from off a carrion-fly—surrounds
That vegetation which is never touched
By any breeze.   The air is thick, and brings
The tainted, subtle sweetness of decay.
Where, yonder, lies the noisome river-course,
There shows a faintly phosphorescent glow.
Long writhing bodies fall and twist and rise,
And one can hear them playing in the mud.

Upon the ruined walls there gleam and shine
The track of those grey, vast monstrosities—
As some gigantic snail had crawled along.

All round the shining bushes waver lines
Suggesting shadows, slight and grey, but full
Of that which makes one nigh to death from fear.

Watch how those awful shadows culminate
And dance in one long wish to hurt the world.

A world that now is past all agony.

BOOK II

ENGLAND RECLAIMED

A BOOK OF ECLOGUES AND OTHER PORTRAITS

To Edith

22 *Dedication*

To you, sad child, upon the darkened stair,
   Poor flaxen foundling of the upper air,
The sweep of whose young wings drew down e'en then
That ugly hate from stupid men and women,
Refined by terror till they could divine
In you th' existence of an inner shrine
Where burnt a flame most rare, while yet their rage
Was heightened by your presence, to this age
So alien that your shape, your very skull
Is now Red Rag to True Blue British bull—
A democratic bull that bends the knee
To naught save money, noise or false simplicity—
To you, who ever fled material halls
And loathed the bloated light on drawing-room walls;
To you, who could pretend no gratitude
For flashing rattle, answering crash, of platitude,
Preferring your own world of tapestry
From words and music woven, where more easily
Your young, flat limbs could move than on a plane
Where, since you loved to read, they burnt again
Your books, or, since you hated cruelties,

And feared such insects, made you kill the flies
That fatly slept or crawled across the glass;
To you, whose pale and legendary face
Still I can see beneath ancestral trees
That greenly shrill with birds, deep drone with bees,
As now you pause among the battlements
And fanes of flowers, to inhale their scents
—Such blossoms as must stoop to you—tall flowers,
Wide-faced, they seemed, that pressed against those
    towers—,
To pluck a blossom with your gothic fingers,
So pointed thin, in which the blood yet lingers
Of tombèd chivalry and arts now dead
—Yet fingers which for us have fashionèd
New instruments of beauty, and have found
New Indias of modern sense and sound;
To you, that magic country's overlord,
Ascetic artist of the painting word,
Your whole life bent to this one, selfless, cause
Of netting beauty with a phrase or pause,
While ev'ry foe to truth makes it his duty
To persecute you in the name of Beauty,
And when you point a new path, leaves his booth
With screams of 'Truth is Beauty, Beauty, Truth,'
Misunderstands, complains, insults and bullies,
Then whips up all the sillies and the dullies
And makes them laugh (for laughter is their lever),
With ev'ry suburb shouting 'Well, I never!';
To you, who earn the ever-righteous hate
Of crowds of giggling, chic cads, I dedicate
These memories of a time when children three
We walked all winter by the white-winged sea
And, under shelter of its lion voice,
Proclaimed the name of Beauty, made our choice.

71

WHEN men were children, and each race was
    young,
The praise of many a hero, bravely sung,
Resounded through each honeycombèd rock
In bee-like droning, smote with sudden shock
The mountain top, where in green-tufted tent
By sweetness drowsed, the shepherd breathes the scent
Of poignant herbs, outprest by scrabbling goat
That quavers to him in a voice remote
As laughter of old men. He stirs not. Past
Him floats the song, to brush the golden mast
Of full-rigg'd fruit trees, where they breast white foam
From fallen petals at their foot, to roam
Through echoing pastures, or invade the woods
Which now reveal, beneath receding floods
Of brutish blackness, goddess-trodden dells
And alleys, whence Apollo shade dispels
With level eye. All animal and furred
Had been that darkness, which with the first word
Man spoke to Man was quelled, by laughter banished;
And yet that fearful darkness has not vanished,
Still lurks within our blood—ape-haunted land
Where ev'ry Stone Age God can still command
With grunting utterance.
                 This chant of love,
This man-made music of the myrtle grove,
Was new then; in its cadence brooded Spring,
The sad months of miraculous blossoming;
Wherever shrilling water met green shade,
Within that laughing, leafy palisade
—As nightingales, that with a diamond tongue
Cut glassy darkness—first the poets sung.

No sooner in these havens had they trod
Before by song they made a Demigod:
All forms of music shared the sacred throne
And Priest and Poet could be seen for one.

.   .   .   .

Heroic figures are now obsolete,
So Demigod and Devil find retreat
In minds of children—as rare beasts and men,
Elsewhere extinct, persist in hill or fen
From man protected—where each form assumes
Gigantic stature and intention, looms
From wind-moved, twilight-woven histories:
For them each flower teems with mysteries.
Thus poems, no less than mythology,
Are imaged through an inner, innocent eye
Preserved from childhood, of a vision clearer,
More true than truth, that brings each object nearer
And draws a strange strength from the hidden God
—For Poetry is the wisdom of the blood,
That scarlet tree within, which has the power
To make dull words bud forth and break in flower.

.   .   .   .

The eye of childhood faithfully records
The destined figures creaking on the boards
Down alleys three—country, abroad and town—
The foreigner, the burgess and the clown:
A false perspective tricked t' appear more deep
Than those dark caskets in which now they sleep,
For children, as they grow, see Fate unfold
These puppets, pack them in their native mould.

.   .   .   .

Now let us wake them: make Miss Mew sit up
To proffer us that kindly, wonted cup

Of tea, with 'just a dash of green tea in it';
Her wrinkled laughter tinkles like a linnet
Among the tea-cups, pecks the ornaments
—The china-cats, the tinselled tournaments,
The ribbon work, which frames in blue and buff
Lord Beaconsfield, and Uncle's box of snuff,
The comrade in his circumnavigation
Of globes grown gay (this fabulous relation
Is often hero of preposterous tales,
Has raided slavers, and has tackled whales
In single combat).   Green eyes open wide,
A white-hair halo foaming like a tide
About her gentle head, she finds escape
In tales of murder, piracy and rape:
Herself believes in these exciting stories
She blends of books she's read and memories,
The while sad mirrors of mahogany
Reflect one sequel to monogamy.
Let Mrs. Hague awake, to hunt her aitches
Down avenues which yet their flight enriches,
Each aitch a rustic goddess, with a crook,
That stirs to life within her green-cut nook:
Let that old soldier, Major Nicodeme,
Provide us with a braggadocio theme.
All these and others let us now implore
To rise, shake on their dust, and speak once more.
Before oblivion's creeping, greedy sea
Shall wash this dust irrevocably
Beyond our reach, let us the past despoil,
Reclaim these precious yards of English soil.

Now watch these phantoms,
How they tremble into being,
Amble, tremble into ample phantoms,
Tumble into their small wants
—Such few desires,
Garden, food, fires.
Watch these phantoms
How they now are being,
Listening . . . . . . hearing,
Looking . . . . seeing,
Loving . . . . fearing,
While to tinge their moods, stiff-jointed moods,
The dumb, the sad, the sunset shadow
Of the old house broods.

Alas, again, the ample phantoms tremble,
Tumble and crumble out of their few needs—
Crumble . . . then crumple up.

25 *Tom*

The farmhand Tom, with his apple and turnip face,
Grumbles, grins and groans through the long summer
hours,
Reviles St. Martin, by whose grace
Thus he must plod through the poppies and cornflowers.
Night is a stretch of dead and drear slumber,
Then up again, and again he must lumber
Into his clothes and away through the park,
Carrying pails,
Must wade through the dark,
Till even the comforting darkness fails,

Tousled and blinking,
Clanking and clinking,
A very robust
Traditional ghost:
>   For clanking and lank
>   The Armoured Knight
>   Rides down the dank
>   Shadows in flight;
>   Grass stiff with frost
>   Shows grey as steel
>   As the Conquering Ghost
>   Clanks down the hill.
>   > Now the first cock crows,
>   > Impudent, frightened, through the dark;
>   > Then a cold wind blows,
>   And that whining dog, Dawn, begins to bark.

Then the Knight in Armour
Passes away,
As the growing clamour
Proclaims, 'It is Day.'
The trees grow taller,
The gate is shut.
The Knight grows smaller,

>   Goes smaller,

>   And out.

26 *Mrs. Hague*

OLD Mrs. Hague,
The Gardener's wife,
Was not to be enclosed in any formulas.
She seems to stand upon a little mound
Of pansies,
>   Primroses,
>   And primulas.

Outlined against the pale blue eye of northern spring,
Heavily planted in this printed muslin beauty
Of clumps and spots and dots and tiger-stripes,
She swelled with ideas and ideals of duty,
Emphatic,
                    Rheumatic.

Mrs. Thatch,
The wife, she was sorry to say,
Of Lord X's gardener
—If such one could call him—
Was silly, town-bred, what Mrs. Hague would call
—Well, she really did not like to say it,
Did not know what to call it;
Shall we say a Ne'er-do-Well?
And all the time the primroses, the wind-flowers
Opened their eyes and pressed their nodding heads
Against her, and the moss seemed ready to
Run up those rugged limbs,
The lichen ready
To crystallize its feathery formations
Along these solid branches.

If not upon this flower-sprinkled mound,
Then Mrs. Hague stood
Pressed in the narrow framework of her door,
And fills it to our minds for evermore.
Out of the slender gaps
Between the figure and its frame,
Was wafted the crusty, country odour
Of new bread,
Which was but one blossom of the hedges
That Mrs. Hague had planted.

For Mrs. Hague was childless,
And so had wisely broken up her life
With fences of her own construction,
Above which she would peer
With bovine grace,
Kind nose, kind eyes
Wide open in wide face.
For

> Monday was Washing Day,
> Tuesday was Baking Day
> Wednesday h'Alfred 'as 'is dinner h'early,
> Thursday was Baking Day again,
> Friday was a busy day, a very busy day,
> And Saturday prepared the way for Sunday,
> Black satin bosoms and a brooch,
> A bonnet and a Bible.

Nor were these all:
There were the other, more imposing, barriers
Of Strawberry Jam in June
And Blackberry Jelly in October:
For each fruit contributed a hedge
To the garden of Mrs. Hague's days.

These fences made life safe for Mrs. Hague;
Each barrier of washing, mending, baking
Was a barricade
Thrown up against being lonely or afraid.
This infinite perspective
—The week, the month, the year—
Showed in the narrow gaps
Between her and the door
As she stood there in the doorway,
Narrow as a coffin.

Oh, who can describe the grace of Mrs. Hague,
A Mrs. Noah limned by Botticelli,
'Mid flowering trees, green winds and pensive flowers;
A Rousseau portrait, inflated by Picasso;
Or seen in summer,
As through a tapestry
Of pool, exotic flower and conifer?

As Daphne was transformed into a tree,
So some old elm had turned to Mrs. Hague,
Thick bole, wide arms and rustic dignity.

27   *Five Drawings of Mr. Hague*

FOR ADRIAN STOKES

I. IN THE PARK

No little mound,
            Printed with garlands of spring flowers,
Serves as a pedestal
For Alfred's memory,
But a bare hillock in a wooded park,
Where graze in clusters
The rouged and dappled deer
—With their large eyes and their thin ankles—,
A miniature Stonehenge
Of which green-aproned Alfred
Was the one vast monolith left standing;
A monosyllabic monolith;
For thirty years of childless married life
Had made him mute.
Alfred loved trees and silence,
And here Mrs. Hague
Dared not disturb him:

For, if Mrs. Hague's home was her castle,
Fortress of home-made jam and new-baked bread,
He ruled
                  The garden,
                              Park,
                                    And potting-shed,
While the hothouse was a studio
In which he worked as artist,
And the peach-houses, the cucumber-frames
Were his also.

Vast monolith he stands,
A landmark many a mile off,
Surveying the trees,
Inspecting leaf and bark and branch—
      For Mrs. Hague
      Is not the only tree he loves:
      Had he wished, then,
      To turn her to a tree?
      Was it a love of trees,
      Or a hope of silence,
      That had once compelled him
      To an Apollonian pursuit of Mrs. Hague?—,
Surveying the trees,
That stand up solitary and tall
Until, becoming rounder, smaller,
Across the fawn-soft slopes
They spin toward the far horizon,
Where foam the woods in green, receding waves—
Gay, singing woods,
In one of which was already growing,
Was, indeed, nearing its full growth,
The boarding for his large, his heavy, coffin.

OH, for words with which
To paint him there from life,
As he stands in the potting-shed
    With the bass, like golden hair,
    And with his insignia,
    Scissors, basket and pruning-knife,
Amid a universe
Of unripe pears and golden bulbs,
    As the stove burns warmly,
    The stove crackles brightly,
And there is a smell of warm wood,
A warm wooden smell as of trees growing
    (Do not ask why the trees are growing,
        Do not ask why the trees are growing).

Here is harboured
The strength of the garden,
Enough growing-power
To make the whole country-side
Flicker
With the red and pink candles of the early spring,
And to illumine again
That little mound
On which for ever in our memories
Stands Mrs. Hague.

3. IN THE HOTHOUSES

IF Mrs. Hague belongs to *Primavera*,
It is to the winter,
A Flemish winter of snow and crackling iron twigs,
That one must assign Alfred.

But Alfred is a master of paradox;
When the English earth is cold
As the lama-ridden uplands of Tibet,
Its temperature subnormal, hungering
To take to itself the lately living, longing
To be warmed and fed
By the annual holocaust of influenza,
When the lake has sheathed its mirror,
And the white giant has put a glass in his eye,
When the shivering margins of the lake
Have wrapped themselves in the feathers of dead swans,
Then I open a glass door,
And in a crystal transparency,
As though within a block of ice,
I find Alfred
—Alfred, white Sultan,
Rajah Brooke of tropic isles—
In one of his dominions;
This one is a forest in the Congo,
A swamp in distant, pear-shaped South America,
The coast of New Guinea
And a jungle in Cochin-China.
    With crimson and damson
    The Nile and the Am'zon
    Emblazon
    This halcyon
    Of growing and blowing
    Warm blossoms and leaves.

4. THE SPELL

HERE the waves of Ceylon
Meet the breakers of the Archipelago—
Breakers trimmed with pearls

And with the eyes of dead sailors—
And out of all this is born
A grinning octaroon of a hybrid
    ('H'Alfred not 'imself to-day,
      Bothered about that 'ere new i-bread').
Here I find him,
Brain, huge stature, and artist fingers
Placed at the entire disposal
Of the most diminutive need
Of an almost invisible blossom.

Here, then, Alfred is a signed Van Eyck
Inserted in a Gauguin panel;
The perfumed and exotic steam
Distilled from Welsh coal—
Heir-at-law
To vast and prehistoric forests—,
From African forests
And Papuan jungles,
Forms round his hairless head
The halo of a saint,
Or the contorted and mottled writhings
Of tropical branch and root
Crown him with Medusa's tresses
    (Can he, perhaps,
    Turn Mrs. Hague to stone
    As well as to a tree,
    And thus make silence doubly sure?)
Fair and rather hairless
He is caught among the variegated tendrils
As in a cobweb,
While the hairy and gnarled arms
Thrust out toward him
Seem the legs of a gigantic,

83

Carnivorous spider,
Which ever drains his strength,
Consumes his years.

Impartially he would distribute praise
Among his turbaned favourites,
Garish or unobtrusive:
'Them's a lovely thing,' he would say,
Indicating a novel invisibility
From the juncture of the Blue and White Niles,
Or pointing out some gargantuan magenta blossom
Newly arrived from the impenetrable forests of Brazil,
'Them's a lovely new thing,'
And he muttered an incomprehensible spell
In horticultural latin.

5. DISCORDANT DAWN

WHEN the cock-crow stretches
The air tight as taut string
Of basso or violin,
Alfred washes and dresses
And hopes for an early spring.

Heavily,
      Warily,
Ever
      So cleverly
He treads through the garden
Where the cold night still lingers,
Though the gold salamander
Flickers its red-crested head
Above the hill yonder.

Now each sharp scent
Is doubly vehement,
Though the frost's white fingers
Pinch the thyme
And bruise the lavender.

An elephant,
                    Pendent
Over the frames,
Where the warm violets glisten
In mauves and magentas—
                    The lips of Infantas—
In brick red or heliotrope,
The robes of Cardinal or Pope,
He murmurs their names
And the flowers listen.

Now a bonfire crackles,
Boldly flashing its golden comb,
Till the acrid scent
Of each frosty plant
Is lost in the firmament.

Mary-Anne

I

Mary-Anne,
                    Wise, simple old woman,
Lived in a patchwork pavilion,
Pitched on an island,
Feeding the piebald and the tartan ducks.

Flotillas of ducks
Lie low in the water,

And Mary-Anne seems
The Duck-King's daughter.
The floating ducks crack up in their arrow-pointed wake
The distorted, silent summer painted in the lake,
And the days disappear
In a leaden stare.

Then Mary-Anne waddles
Through the evening cool,
And a smell of musk
Lingers by the pool,
For the trembling fingers of the honeysuckle
Wring out the blue and the dew-drenched dusk.

At night the pavilion
Is hung by a silver cord
That the nightingales plait
With their intercoiling song.
Within, Mary-Anne mutters
The Word of the Lord,
Till the candle gutters,
As the summer sighs outside
And taps
At the shutters.

2

The silver-threaded wire
With which the nightingales
Suspended her pavilion
Was not the sole support it seemed:
For there was a direct attachment,
An umbilical cord to Heaven.
Her web-footed world
Teemed with four-leafed clovers,

With tea-leaves, cards, new moons,
And every sort of augury.
Not frightened, never in the least,
But seeing things,
Constantly,
For was she not
The Seventh Child of a Seventh Child
Born under Venus,
Had she not seen the Blue Man ride
Away, the bleak night that the late lord died?

Opposite on the shore
Was the Cedar Avenue,
Where fallen fragrance hushed the footsteps,
And there,
Quite often of an evening,
Mary-Anne could see
The Cavalier lord walking,
More conventional in death than in life ever,
Carrying his handsome head beneath an out-turned arm.
It was he who had done all this for Mary-Anne,
　　Who had made the lake and given it countless things
　　　　to mirror;
　　Who had made the broken flights of steps,
　　The balustrades, the floating-terraces
　　And colonnades, wherein Italian winds
　　Whispered and sang their arias—
　　Winds he had netted centuries ago
　　In the plumed grottoes of a Roman garden—
　　And statues that the years had fretted
　　To limbless, eyeless, lipless lepers.
It was he, too, who had planted the park with hawthorns
That prance like red and white chessmen
Through the chequered springtime.

3

In the winter her pavilion
Was a tent of swansdown.
The windows tightly closed
Showed through their brittle yellow ice
A fern, and cubèd walls.
The wild geese thrust their long necks
Out into the cold air above,
And the white feathers drifted up to the window.
Then the Family would come down,
Like so many cats after the birds, she always said.
The snowflakes would sway down,
And thud,
> Thud,
>> Thud
>>> Would sound the falling pheasants.

29 *Mr. and Mrs. Nutch*

For Sacheverell

I. MRS. NUTCH

Deep in the summer wood
Under a patch of sky
Crouched Mrs. Nutch,
Sworn foe, harsh enemy
Of every cobweb, mouse and Roman Catholic:
Crouched Mrs. Nutch,
An ancient owl in spectacles,
An owl diminishing, alas, from year to year,
Slipping down out of sight
Behind the warm shelter of an apricot tree
That billowed green leaves over golden stars.

For Mrs. Nutch and this tree,
Though she tended it
And it bore fruit for her,
Were marching in contrary directions.
The tree grew taller
As Mrs. Nutch grew nearer to the ground,
Whence one sprang,
And by which the other
Was soon to be swallowed up.

In the very height of summer,
When the smell of hay
Wandered down the long lanes of the wood,
Banished the damp smell of the bracken;
When the long, triumphant evenings
Planted their scarlet banners
In the very citadel of the hostile night,
Then Mrs. Nutch would stand in the doorway,
While her spectacles flashed back
The sun's victorious adieu,
Or would peep over
The spires of the campanulas,
As the evening winds
Ring their blue and white carillons—
Bloated capitalist campanulas,
Which to prosper
She must feed with blood.

.   .   .   .

Few were her recreations:
There was the 'Ebenezer'—
Stony acropolis of every mining-village—,
She could ponder, perhaps,
On the Pope of Rome
Or the Whore of Babylon:

Read a passage she had found
In the newspaper
Aloud to incurious Mr. Nutch:
Then there was a musical box that tinkled 'Carmen',
Combing out luxuriant tresses with its golden teeth,
And her own cracked quavering
Of the 'Hallelujah Chorus'—
A treat, this one, for others
As much as for herself,
To be served out to children
Instead of cakes or sweets.
After it, she would lie back,
Panting, in her chair,
As an owl pants in a holly-bush.
Sombre fires flickered in her eye,
While she sat there exhausted:
And then, suddenly,
As an aeroplane takes flight,
She would soar again after a fluttering, lustrous cobweb

2. MR. NUTCH

MR. NUTCH,
Brown-bearded bear,
Chased the scamps of boys through fruit trees.
'Scamps', he called them,
But it was a serious affair,
Breaking down the palings
And Stealing Property.

> Clumsily he would grab and ramble,
> Angrily he would dart and grumble,
> Heavily he would sway and shamble
>   After the nimble boys.

He would stumble among the trees,
Full-branchèd apples

That sagged beneath their rosy swags,
Or crabs that trailed their bitter-sweet rockets
Across the crisp autumn air.

Bombardments of apples
And impudent laughter
Met Mr. Nutch
Where'er he might wander,
His crinkled boots crusted with crystals
Under the glittering cobweb-tangled autumn.
(Oh,
     If only Mrs. Nutch
          Could have tidied up the season,
          What a different autumn it would have been,
          With its neatly piled pyramids of apples,
          Sorted according to size and colour,
          Even the branches graded,
          Placed symmetrically
          One above another,
          The grass dry, well-aired
          And of an even height!)
But, as it was,
There, heavily trudging,
Angry and out of breath
Mr. Nutch must grab and ramble
From one walled garden to another.
At his approach
The birds would flutter in the fruit nets,
Bump and struggle in the fruit nets;
Each small bird that pecked the honeyed heart
Of golden or grape-blushing plum,
Was in reality a vulture
Feeding on Mr. Nutch's entrails—
Mr. Nutch,

That Prometheus bound to an orchard.
But the birds would flutter and struggle,
For Mr. Nutch
Was the natural enemy of every bird,
However soft or gaudy-feathered,
Just as Mrs. Nutch
Was the sworn foe
Of every cobweb,
          Mouse and
               Roman Catholic.

3. MRS. NUTCH, MR. NOYES AND MYSELF

MRS. NUTCH's constant expectation
Of the second coming,
A pleasurable but revengeful picnic,
Where the proud were, perhaps, more to be degraded
Than the humble exalted,
Disturbed my nights,
Filled them with the lion-mouthed roarings
Of drums and trumpets.

And so I lay awake,
Hearing the owls
Hooting round in the darkness,
While ever so far away
A loud-pounding goods-train
Lumbered along the southern path to London—
Lumbered along, had I but known it then,
To the precise rhythm of Mr. Alfred Noyes' verse,
For every train at night
Sings its own song
As surely as a bird.

.   .   .   .

Then silence,
Mr. Noyes had finished;
The owl still snored,
Deep, ever so deep
In the holly,
Heigh-ho! in the holly.

4. MRS. NUTCH IN HER ARM-CHAIR

No wonder she was tired, she thought,
Working her fingers off, as one might say,
Working her very fingers off,
Every day except the Seventh Day.
For, ancient owl in spectacles,
She must sweep down continually
Upon her rightful prey,
The velvet-footed, clockwork-moving mice
That tittered so teasingly
Behind the panelling
Upon the Sabbath
    (Oh, they knew, they knew),
Or she must organize a battue
Against the spider
In all his wicked, silky machinations.

Moping Fred

I. MOPING FRED

Fred Nutch,
  The final though not favourite offspring
Of the warrior pair,
Would in himself have blended,
One supposes,

Two such royal strains—
    Male gun and female broomstick—,
But such, emphatically,
Was not the case.
He would not sweep or shoot:
                         Instead
He hid within the wood
Or *Read*
    Among the roses
        (Oh, you could see it in his face, you could),
    A process widely noticed, rightly recognized
As 'Moping'—
        Hence
        'Moping Fred.'

2. IN A NUTSHELL

YOUNG Nutch, They said,
Would never be the Man
His Father was:
Because
    He did not know how to manage,
Carried no weight
In Evidence against the Boys—
    Straddling across the creaking limbs of ancient apple
        trees,
    Hanging their coronals of laughter
    Untidily among the branches
    As they climbed and clambered
    Up in green cradles, golden bowls of light,
    Clashing their coronals against the tiding silver of the
        songs
    Of birds that sang more easily again
    Because of the deceiving voice of that Delilah autumn
    Receiving them into the heart of her false spring—,

Would not even help his Father
Pursue the scamps—
    Scamps *he* called them—
Through the golden corridors of the orchard
    (Clumsily Mr. Nutch must ramble,
    Angrily and alone must grumble,
    Heavily and alone must shamble
        After the nimble boys)—
Would not slit open the soft,
Warm, silver stomach of a rabbit,
    Though its faunal ears were matted with blood,
Would not crucify an owl upon a barn door
Or help the old man out in any way:
Was,
    To put it in that tooth-splintering
    Yet well-chewed platitude, a nutshell,
    Too fond of Moping
    And of Reading Books,
        Charges synonymous
        And polyonymous,
        Almost as serious
As Breaking Down the Palings and Stealing Property.

31   *Mr. and Mrs. Goodbeare*

FOR THOMAS BALSTON

I. ELEGY FOR MR. GOODBEARE

Do you remember Mr. Goodbeare, the carpenter,
Godfearing and bearded Mr. Goodbeare,
Who worked all day
At his carpenter's tray,
Do you remember Mr. Goodbeare?

95

Mr. Goodbeare, that Golconda of gleaming fable,
Lived, thin-ground between orchard and stable,
Pressed thus close against Alfred, his rival—
Mr. Goodbeare, who had never been away.

Do you remember Mr. Goodbeare,
Mr. Goodbeare, who never touched a cup?
Do you remember Mr. Goodbeare,
Who remembered a lot?
    Mr. Goodbeare could remember
        When things were properly kept up:
    Mr. Goodbeare could remember
        The christening and the coming-of-age:
    Mr. Goodbeare could remember
        The entire and roasted ox:
    Mr. Goodbeare could remember
        When the horses filled the stable,
And the port-wine-coloured gentry rode after the
        tawny fox:
    Mr. Goodbeare could remember
        The old lady in her eagle rage,
            Which knew no bounds:
    Mr. Goodbeare could remember
        When the escaped and hungering tiger
Flickered lithe and fierce through Foxton Wood,
When old Sir Nigel took his red-tongued, clamouring
        hounds,
And hunted it then and there,
        As a Gentleman Should.

Do you remember Mr. Goodbeare,
Mr. Goodbeare who never forgot?

Do you remember Mr. Goodbeare,
That wrinkled and golden apricot,
Dear, bearded, godfearing Mr. Goodbeare
Who remembered remembering such a lot?

Oh, do you remember, do you remember,
As I remember and deplore,
That day in drear and far-away December
When dear, godfearing, bearded Mr. Goodbeare
Could remember
No more?

2. MR. AND MRS. GOODBEARE

MR. GOODBEARE'S parlour was a paradise
Of polished wood, a haven of joinery,
A heaven of varnish.
There were brackets, shelves, shields
And cupboards, with ferns traced on them
By his artistry,
And even wooden vases, turned
So beautifully, and full of dried, dull grasses,
Tied with dusty ribbons,
That rustled suffocatingly
In the dry wind from under the door.
Fantastic flights of Mr. Goodbeare's imagination,
Cricket-bats combined with dragons,
And improbable bows and loops,
Framed-in the almost legendary
Topiary of beard and whisker—
Tied in True-lover's Knots,
In which Mr. Goodbeare's friends
Had at one time extravagantly—
If elegantly—indulged.

. . . .

G

Mrs. Goodbeare herself appeared no mean feat of turnery,
As she creaked into the room
In her best black satin dress.
The lines on her face,
Of hairy yellow wood just cut,
Had been incised, perhaps,
By Mr. Goodbeare's verbal saw,
Just as his actual one
Had roughly shaped her figure.
Carved from one tree-trunk
She appeared,
Save for a golden-gleaming tooth,
A weird, wild tooth
That flashed in sympathy or anger.
Mrs. Goodbeare was a diplomat
And played off Mrs. Hague 'gainst Mrs. Nutch—
Yet sometimes I feared that Mrs. Goodbeare
Thought that dear, bearded, godfearing Mr. Goodbeare
Remembered remembering
Too much.

3. MR. GOODBEARE AT WORK

UNDER the shade
Of the elder-bushes,
In the speckled glade,
Where the thrush-coloured toads crouch
About to spring,
Where the toad-coloured thrushes
Learn to sing,
To shake their notes
As do Prima-Donnas
From white, fat throats;
When the tulips flaunt
Their proud bandannas,

And the cuckoos haunt
Us with mocking hosannahs,
Then, if you pass
Betwixt orchard and stable,
You can hear the saw shriek
From the Carpenter's table.
With saw and with plane,
The colour of rain,
He turns the old trees into shelves; or, again,
Into hives for the bees
That seek golden ease
In the cups of the flowers
Battered down by the showers,
Blue-cold as the claw
Of the plane or the saw
That make for cattle a pen,
Or fashion coffins for men.

.   .   .   .   .   .

But if Mr. Goodbeare
Planes the planks, and prepares
Caskets for men's skeletons,
Alfred for this atones,
And takes him unawares
By planting flowers
For Mr. Goodbeare's dry and tirèd bones.

4. MR. GOODBEARE'S COTTAGE

How Mrs. Goodbeare
Could ever have contrived
In that Sahara of dry grasses and dry wood
To suffer 'from rheumaticks somethink dreadful'
Remains her secret
—The only one which Destiny allowed her.

For Mr. Goodbeare, being a carpenter,
Enjoyed immensely the effect
Of windows,
                    Tightly closed
                            And nicely, very nicely, painted,
Of well-turned wood,
                            Well-seasoned,
And of painted putty
                            (Oh, the painted putty!)
While the neatly-fitting panes
Afforded him an exquisite sensation,
Unknown but to his trade.
The glass panes gave a gloss
To anything behind,
And brought to mind—
                            French Polish,
Zenith of evolutional anthropoid achievement.
Then there were always plants,
An aspidistra or two, behind the ice
That shut them from the northern world.

        Sometimes the windows looked
        Like mountain waters rilling over ferns,
        Sometimes the fleshy red lip of a cactus
        Touched them to strange exoticism,
        Or, again, the sun flashed down on one
        Till it resembled
The golden tooth
That gleamed in sympathy or anger.
No air was there within—
        Except the dry wind creeping
        And squeezing and moaning and whining under the
            door
While the house was sleeping—

For no window was ever open,
    Neither upon the glittering steel flowers of the frost,
    Nor on those fantastic blossoms
    Spun by the sun with aid of summer rain
    Among most ordinary green leaves,
    Nor on those magic crystal lilies
    Which the rain beats up
    Upon hard paths
    And which dissolve and die in blossoming,
    Nor ever on the cornucopia
    Of summer noons weighty with full-blown roses,
    When the Red Admirals ride smoothly
    Down the painted tide of petals,
    Furl their shuddering sails
    Deep in the harbour of the flowers' heart—
But, for her, only on to valleys biblical,
Valleys that still were
The Church-of-England haunt and habitat
Of Baal and Jael
      ('Tis true the wooden pin
      Excited *his* professional interest too),
Of flaunting, dizened Jezebel
And strings of generating names—
Nimrod, Omri, Nehemiah and Melchisedek:
For him, on to dry lawns of rattling, pressed grasses,
On to perspective-twisting pastures
Of the things remembered,
And now growing larger as they roll away
Toward the horizon, or upon
Desiccated forests of artful fretwork,
Or lone logs of wood, unseasoned and unpainted,
Still rooted in the earth—
    Logs which would cut up beautiful
    Into shelves: then into boxes, into frames,

Just dainty odds and ends,
So very handy, and the fruit of skill;
Meantime the unremembering, unambitious dove
Croons languorously
High up in Mr. Goodbeare's elm tree.

32 *Mr. and Mrs. Southern*

For Hazel Lavery

I. MRS. SOUTHERN'S ENEMY

A T dusk it is—
    Always at dusk—
    I seem to see again
That grey typhoon we knew as Mrs. Southern,
Spinning along the darkened passages,
Watching things, tugging things,
Seeing to things,
     And putting things to rights.

Oh, would that the cruel daylight, too,
Could give us back again
Dear Mrs. Southern,
Dear selfless, blue-lipped Mrs. Southern,
Cross, mumbling and transparent Mrs. Southern,
With her grey hair,
    Grey face,
      And thinly-bitter smile,
In wide blue skirt, white-spotted, and white apron;
On the very top of her head she carried a cap,
An emblem of respect and respectability, while
As though she were a Hindu charmer of snakes,
Her hair lay coiled and tame at the back of her head.

But her actual majesty was really the golden glory,
Through which she moved, a hurrying fly
Enshrined in rolling amber,
As she spun along in a twisting column of golden atoms,
A halo of gold motes above and about her,
A column of visible, virtuous activity.
Her life was a span of hopeless conflict,
For she battled against Time,
That never-vanquished and invisible foe.

She did not recognize her enemy,
She thought him Dust:
But what is Dust,
Save Time's most lethal weapon,
His faithful ally and our sneaking foe,
Through whom Time steals and covers all we know,
The very instrument with which he overcame
Great Nineveh and Rome and Carthage,
Ophir and Trebizond and Ephesus,
Now deep, all deep, so deep in dust?
 Even the lean and arid archæologist,
 Who bends above the stones, and peers and ponders,
 Will, too, be his one day.
Dust loads the dice,
Then challenges to play,
Each layer of dust upon a chair or table
A tablet to his future victory.
And Dust is cruel, no victory despising,
However slight,
And Dust is greedy, eats the very bones;
So that, in the end, still not content
With trophies such as Helen of Troy,
Or with the conquering golden flesh of Cleopatra

(She, perhaps, understood the age-long battle,
For did she not prefer to watch her pearl
Dissolve in amber wine,
Thus herself enjoying
Its ultimate disintegration,
Than let Dust conquer such a thing of beauty?
Was not the asp, fruit-hidden,
The symbol of such understanding?),
He needs must seize on Mrs. Southern,
Poor mumbling, struggling, blue-lipped Mrs. Southern,
For Dust is insatiate and invincible.

2. TWILIGHT

THROUGH long and intimate association
With the objects under her protection,
Mrs. Southern had the air
Of being in league with inanimate objects,
Conspirator with chair and table,
Sentient wall, inquisitive-eyed portrait.

So, when I hear faint creakings from a board
Or in the twilight the muffled hurry and harry
And worry and flurry of something that scurries along,
I wonder what it is, and whether Mrs. Southern wanders
And works and suffers, yet bound to chair and table;
For she was always there,
Whenever you looked round.
She was there all the time:
Had been there the whole time
While you had called her:
Had been for fifty years,
Standing there, looking after things.

Is there, I wonder, is there in the guilty dust
Some indecipherable message
Written with accusing but invisible finger?
By a cruel fate, herself now actual part
Of that same foe she fought for a whole lifetime,
Surely she would betray him if she could,
As she watches him and his ally,
Night, the Black Panther,
Stealing on velvet paws
Through the long corridors,
Then slink into the garden where the red mouths tremble
Till all the points of colour crumble,
Till the young wind-god is woken
And battles with them as his muscles strengthen,
By his day-long drowsiness forsaken?
Now the glowing glass below is broken,
Now the plunging images are shaken,
And the dying shadows lengthen,

> Lengthen,
> > Lengthen.

3. MR. SOUTHERN IN THE MARKET GARDEN

MR. SAMUEL SOUTHERN, though he looked the part,
Toyed in no myrtle grove,
Nor was static in the forefront
Of any oriental landscape.
It is always on a summer day
 (Then were no days
 Save summer days,
 Or a few days of swansdown,
 When the old elms
 Held high their hundred antlers,
 Now spun of glass and silver,
 Into the brittle blue of winter)

That I see him, sitting before a table,
Making up accounts in a vast book,
A local god, who blossoms on this stone platform
Beneath the shelter of a tulip tree,
Tallying life with death.
An emanation from the soil is he,
And yet a miniature god in his miniature heaven;
Behind him (the cloud posed for his godship)
Showed the gleaming, faded Orangery
Through whose mackerel-cloudy yet transparent scales
Could still be detected
    (For chiming bells are due as much,
    As much decreed, to minor gods,
    As rolling guns for the salute of native princes)
The sad, pale ringing
Of a thousand waxen bells,
Gently swinging, nodding, ringing
High in the dark and leafy air.

There sat the god, and for the heaven he ruled,
Lay sprawled across the park, the old square garden
Full of the feathered trunks of apple trees,
Whose fluttered leaves ride, small cupids on a golden
      breeze.
Here Mr. Southern, rustic deity,
Could tot up to his satisfaction
The local lives and deaths,
The christenings, the marriages, the funerals
For which he customarily supplied—
    According to th' inexorable laws
    Of birth and death—
    Or let us say of Supply and Demand—
Appropriate floral decorations.

And oh, he cherished a Shakespearian appetite
For every word of sexton and of verger,
And for each gesture of the undertaker!

4. NO FLOWERS BY REQUEST

UNDER the apple trees
The garden was divided
Into four quarters,
Each box-edged and trim.
One quarter, thus, was given up to funerals,
And nominally one to christenings,
Though, actually, interchangeable,
　　Haunted by every damp, albino ghost
　　In its own season,
　　　　By all the decadent and spectral blossoms
　　　　From fainting snowdrop to the weak narcissus,
　　　　From fat, white daisies
　　　　To white asters,
　　While, worse than such moist ghosts
Were those dry, lifeless, stillborn, chilly flowers
That never can tremble and flutter as other flowers do like
　　　　a bird on the breeze,
But can only quake and rustle and rattle.
And then, in a Good Year,
　　An influenza or a typhoid year,
He did a wun'erful lot o' trade,
　　He told me,
In white chrysanthemums—
Nothing like white chrysanthemums
To give the rich but cold look
That was wanted.

Then there was a quarter given up to weddings—
　　　But a lot liked white for weddings too, Mrs. Southern
　　　　　for example—
And that final quarter for assorted flowers,
Suited to bazaars and jubilees,
Victorious wars and vicarage jumble-sales.
For these he recommended something patriotic,
Geraniums and lobelias,
　　　　　　　　　With a touch
　　　　　　　　　　　　Of white. . .

33　　　　　　　*Phoebe Southern*

I. PHOEBE SOUTHERN

IT was not
　　By Phoebe's hair of northern sunlight,
　　　Weaving pale gold, pale green, all caught in gold,
That one would recognize her,
　　　Nor by her figure
　　　That like Daphne seemed
　　　About to change into a lithe young tree
　　　Of earliest spring, whose shrill green curls,
　　　Unfolding like the purest melodies,
　　　Are weighted down with coral buds and bells—
　　　　　All swinging on the branches, gently ringing
　　　　　In time with the deep-throated hornpipes,
　　　　　The flings, the jigs and rigadoons
　　　　　That are the favourite tunes
　　　　　Of English birds, adventurous
　　　　　Wave-braving mariners—
　　　Nor by her green eyes' animal, swift flash,
　　　Forswearing such arboreal temptation,
But by the crooning of her dove-like laughter,

That fluttering laughter,
Laughter of birds high up, content in their jade summer,
The laughter of a naiad,
As she flits like a dryad through the drowsing woods,
As she drifts down the orchards
With their anchored clouds,
Or across the lawns, like Leda for the moment
Enfolded, swallowed up in the flashing, frothing feathers
Of those proud swans, the fountains;
Still laughing is she,
Always questioning, always laughing,
Her voice carrying always, even in its laughter,
The upward-speeding, arrow-angle of a question.

2. SILVER LANCES

PHOEBE saw him as he tilted at the Turk's Head,
Riding low, stooping under the branches of the trees,
Half Robin Hood and half Crusader,
In his green uniform a-jingle with silver mail.

She saw him as he rode by at the gallop
Look toward her, turning in his saddle,
He had seen her and she saw him as he rode by at the gallop,
And the moving and the ripple of his chest now that his
    arm made ready
To tilt at the Turk's Head with his long lance of silver,
While in turn the sun tilted at him as he rode,
Tilting long shimmering lances down at him through golden
    branches.

It was
    After the Flower Show and the music and the uniforms,
    After the flowers, music and its furbelows,
        The changing sunlight and the waving trees,

After the charging lancers with their lances flashing,
After the tents, the booths and Punch-and-Judy shows,
After the slow wandering, slow wondering,
After the shifting and the tangle
    Of trees and flowers and tents and gaily moving
      people
    Upon the vegetable-scented, aphrodisiac breeze,
After the flashing brass and the heroic trumpets,
    Swooping like gold-billed eagles down the wind,
After the conjuror and the rustic magic,
    The green, the red and then the golden jangle
    Of buzzing tunes amid the fluttering leaves,
    That, laughing in the dusk, she met him,
That martial, moustached, stiff ghost of a cocoanut,
Sergeant Maypole,
With his matted hair and white teeth,
His wooden, hairy face and cocoanut-like muscles—
Though to her he was that glamorous crusader,
Romantic, amorous, Robin-Hood Crusader,
Set for eternity amid the music
Of trumpets under trees.

34   *Mr. and Mrs. Kembley*

I. LUKE KEMBLEY IN SEPTEMBER

THE autumn was Luke Kembley's season,
   October was Luke Kembley's month—
Though there was a lot to be said for September,
    A nice fine September,
Hung with red apples and with golden pears,
    A nice fine September,
Hung with glistening cobwebs;
    A nice fine September,

When hilltop and meadow were full of the smell of the cabbage,
And when his stout shooting-boots
First plodded down the furrows
Of the fecund earth.

Stealthily crouching, he would stalk
Between the golden forts
And crenellated towers of summer,
Thrown up by the sweating binders
Against the invading Autumn—
For it was always a late harvest—,
Between the leafy avenues of the root-crops,
Between the frozen waves
Of sea-green cabbages,
Off which the marble-veinèd dew would rattle,
As he passed,
Like the spray from breakers.
Sometimes his boot
Would crunch and crackle on a root,
As, later, would the strong teeth
And rhythmic jaws
Of the devouring cattle;
Then the plump birds would whir
Almost from beneath his foot,
Whir through the butterfly-hung air
With the rushing sound of an ogre's indrawn breath.

But in September
The Farmers were the trouble.
    Farmers were never contented,
        Farmers thought they had the right to everything,
        Farmers grumbled,
            Farmers took the law into their own
                hands,
And you could not stop them:

III

So that,

> Though there was a lot to be said for September
>> (A nice fine September),

October was Luke Kembley's month.

2. AND OCTOBER

October was Luke Kembley's month,
When the golden castles of the corn
Had been slighted by the roundhead autumn.
Then, red as the berries that grow
On the hawthorn hedges—oh!
He could walk after pheasants with a gun.

Day and night,
Spring and summer long,
He would lurk in the woods,
Eating bread and cheese
And never resting,
Preparing for October.
He would guard the sacred birds,
He would give them to drink,
He would offer up grain at their wooden altars:
He would even secure
Their effigies of straw
Within low branches,
So that,

> In the dark,

A panicked poacher
Could fire for ever at a sitting pheasant,
And no bird would fall.

In the night he would stalk the running sounds
Pursue the flickering lights:
Then the blue tapestries

Would rustle sullenly, swaying
Puffed out upon the breath
Of the lank,
The dank, green ghosts
Of dead forests

But
    October was the month,
    When the northern air is crystal
And the berries grow all red upon the hedges—oh!,
When the tall trees grow antlers,
    And the three-prong'd leaves of the bracken
    Undulate on the pure air
    Just as the triple tails of imperial goldfish
    Wave through their transparent element;
    When even the Sun,
    Magnificent Inca,
    Wraps himself each evening
    For his ceremonial farewell
    In gigantic pheasant-feathers.
Then Luke Kembley's breath
Lingered behind him on the air,
As he walked back through the dusk
To find the sharp fingers of the fire
Gilding Mrs. Kembley
In the cottage on the hill.

But now through the cold and the long Octobers
The frost-flowers grow on the stiff stone borders,
And the dark winds blow
Through the lepers' window,
And the Parson blows his nose
As he passes in,
And the sky above
Is as dull as sin——

113

And the poachers trample down the dying woods,
And the pheasants are few,
  The pheasants are few.

3. CIRCLES

THE very house seemed circular,
A beehive or a top,
While Mrs. Kembley
Was not only wife
To Mr. Kembley—
Far, far more than that.
Her very face and build and engineering
Shouted her 'Female' to his 'Male';
The same concentric circles,
     Highly coloured,
But used quite differently,
Arranged so dexterously,
Turned out into two lots,
Two continents,
Connected by a scarcely visible isthmus;
Or she might be an hour-glass,
     With a head above it.
So round was she, upon her two small feet
She seemed to spin, spin more than move,
Among the watery pleasances of her kitchen,
While beyond the open door,
Out in the garden,
     That lay scratched upon the hilltop
     Like a pattern made with a stick upon the sands,
All the flowers were either round and sweet
     And highly coloured,
Or, gently feathered like a pheasant,
Spun upon a pleasant breeze.

THE house was fortunately warm, a wigwam
Woven of fur and feather;
Had it been cold,
It would have been a mortuary,
A morgue for every feather, fur and fin.
There were feathers in vases
Feathers in patterns hung up on the walls,
Feathers under glass,
And a feathered fire-screen.
Even the flames that this screen caged
Became diabolically mimetic,
And shook gay feathers from the grate,
Unfolded plumy tails.
Then there were innumerable fragments, finely mounted,
Of the beasts of the field as well as of birds of the air,
And huge fishes, with their fixed bright eyes,
Like those of paralytics,
That could yet contrive to catch,
From their glass houses,
Which boasted imitation reeds and ferns,
The bird-quick eye of Mrs. Kembley,
As she spun, bustled, opened and shut the doors.
Indeed, they swam right up the walls,
And mouthed aridly at her from the frieze;
While outside, in the kitchen, in the airy larder,
Through which there ever flew
A shrill, blue-feathered, little Alpine wind,
Were more birds, more dead birds,
Real birds, tied by their coral feet to rails,
More fish, all shining, damp and speckled,
Chequered or mail-coated,
With a piteous fin yet twitching,
Cradled in green rushes and long grass,

Just as they were brought in—
Rushes and green grass that cruelly parodied
Those green, faint-waving weeds
That had been shade
For all their glittering courtships,
Those weeds that rippled in the stream's clear play.
 (This parody consisting
 In the want of movement
 In things that should, it seemed,
 Move naturally and imperceptibly:
 Just thus is death the parody of sleep.)
But Mrs. Kembley spun about
And bustled through her mortuary,
Her small feet tapping out
Quick staccato patterns on the hard, stone pavers,
There was much to do——
And the sound of the golden threshing
Was borne up from the field below.

5. EVENING

Of an evening, Mrs. Kembley
Would wait for Mr. Kembley on the hill—
Waiting a little frightened,
For the woods under were so still,
     So still,
For the mist crept up the nearer valleys,
Whispering white and chill;
Down in them something murmured
 (Was it the distant rill?),
More dusky grew the long green alleys,
And the voices of the woods stabbed, sharp and shrill.
Then the nearest light winked yonder,
 Miles down, by the mill,

And the Roman road ran straight and silent,
Empty and waiting, it seemed, along the hill.
She knew there was no reason to be frightened,
There was nothing for her to fear.
The valleys thus were always whitened
By the mist; the cruel wood voices sounded shrill
Always when all else was still——
But darkness was sidling near,

                  And nearer,
And Mrs. Kembley waited on the hill. . . .

35   *Grand Finale*

THE FLOWER SHOW

IF I must leave the faces that I love,
Let it be when every dove
    Is crooning, swinging in the soft June trees,
And roses ride on every breeze:
    Thus would I love the faces that I leave
    And need not so much grieve.

Vast yellow mushrooms, tents are pitched
Beneath tall shadow-weaving trees
    That wring long hands
    And flutter their green fingers,
Amazed at so much boisterous hilarity,
While the grass, blue hair of wood-nymphs,
Displays broad yellow partings, leading to the tents;
Partings made yellow with the trip and tramp
Of boots, such stiff and torturing best-boots.
Now, in the yellow fungoid shade within,
So thick a crowd attempts to move
That all the bodies merging into one

Make movement slow and vastly ponderous—
    As though an elephant
    Both filled the tent
And strove to trample through it—
While this beast, more fabulous
    Than any howdah'd favourite
    Kneeling in grey salaam
Before some proud, some emerald-crested peacock of a Rajah,
Supports a thousand shifting heads,
    Each with a bowler hat or bonnet
    Jauntily perched upon it.
And all these faces, shining faces full of wonder,
Perpetually are shifting, blossoming anew
    (And yet not only do these faces shift and blossom,
    But some drop down each year,
    Withered as though by magic, nothing left of them—
    Only another youthful head blossoms more gaily
    There, where the old one nodded for so long,
    Not even a small gap now showing to record it),
And all these faces, shining faces full of wonder,
Open into fresh patterns of contentment,
As they peer and stare and let the scene
Drum through them, permeate them with its marvels;
    Intent with both eyes and one ear,
    For now the fanfare changes
    To a rhythmic drone;
    The other ear is bent to catch
    The succulent spirals of the tune,
    Sea-fruit up-thrown against this littered shore
    By the brassy ocean's snore.
Such tunes have lives as much as mortals,
For, just as gods breathe into men
The life that grows, then flows, then ebbs away,
Thus does a tune derive its life from man;

And this dead tune,
This empty, broken shell
Matches the relics that we see about us,
The bits of fur and feather, and the sequined
Finery of such a festival,
Where dance dead fashions with a clownish elegance
Through yellow air, scented symphonically
With hot red roses, with carnations,
Prize onions and prize potatoes,
In their various armours of gold, their armours of purple,
With the smell of hairy, yellow boards
Pressing down upon hot, yellow grass.
And through this gloom, and through the blatant sounds
Of unearned and departed glory,
The warm, contented faces
Smile, speak a word, or hang above
The bouquets and the nosegays and the posies
That wilt in jampots and inferior vases,
Carefully consider horticultural triumphs
    That singly ride
    In pride as specimens.

Among these happy hanging gardens
Of red and rustic faces,
    Which hide few fancies
    And are round and open as the pansies
That tied in little crumpled velvet bouquets
Curl up their petals, there are many that we know.

But, as the flowers in the yellow tent,
These bouquets, and these nosegays and their posies,
Wilt, hour by hour, in their inferior vases,
So wilt and wither these poor, happy heads, now bent
Above the blossoms, year by year.

And as they stoop, and bend, and form their judgment
With careful and appraising eye,
So, surely, for a moment I could see
God's face bent down, and peering curiously
Above these faces, wide and open as the pansies'
Faces, which have no doubts, and hide no fancies.

If I must leave these faces that I love,
And it is not when every dove
Is crooning, swinging in the soft June trees,
And roses ride on every breeze,
Then let me take of them my last farewell
At this sad, this gay, this flowery festival;
So would I love the faces that I leave
And need not so much grieve.

Sound out, proud trumpets,
And you, bugles, blow
Over the English Dead,
Not slain in battle, in no sense sublime
These rustic figures caught at last by Time,
And yet their blood was warm and red
As any roses that in England grow
To these anonymous armies of the dead.
Blow, bugles, blow;
Sound out, proud trumpets, let your brazen thunder
Wake them to make them pass
Before us under the wide sky.
Thunder, drums and trumpets, thunder,
Wake them, to rise from where they lie
Under,
Under,
Under
The green grass,
Under the wide grey sky.

Miss Mew

I. A FEATHER TAPESTRY

How few
The things we knew
About Miss Mew!

She was a delicate feather blown out of a pastel past,
Upon some shattering gale
Of which no one was ever told the nature.

There had been a gap, a long gap, and then
Pitching upon some dull, some blunt
Relentless gust of the east wind
She had drifted hither,
This delicate feather;
Here, where the waves ruffle their white plumage
At her all the winter,
Here, where the sky brushes the blue tops of the houses
All the winter
With its grey feathers, black or yellow feathers.

Age could not undermine her grace,
But only fashioned her more lightly,
Gave her a white halo,
And made her green eyes larger
In her white, small face,
So lightly carved her feet, that when she walked,
She drifted like a feather adown the wind,
Drifting among these other brutal and gigantic feathers
That buffeted and battered her
In the unreal and yellow light of English winter.

2. MISS MEW-AD-VINCULA

WHAT chains, then, what weights were there
To bind her down
—This feather floating on the wind—
To the substantial winter of her life?

An undefinable, slight accent in her speech,
Drifting down it lightly as a feather in the wind;
No education and much knowledge;
A carriage accident, political convictions;
A love of stage and dancing, and of scenes
Where under the green and sickly flicker of the gaslight
Pranced Taglioni on her bird-swift toes
Leading a floating and angelic host
Of swooning swans and pirouetting nymphs;
Allegèd friendship with the hook-nosed Gounod
Among the painted pinks and blues,
The pampered but rebellious palm-trees
Of the early Riviera,
So that to our minds
All the trinkets in her house
Tinkled when she spoke or moved
To the rhythm of the Jewel-Song;
And that rare atmosphere which she distilled in talk,
An atmosphere both bourgeois and bohemian
Combined of high-kicks and home-truths,
Flirtation, elegance, and laughter,
But with the gilded pawnshop and the golden ginshop
Always round the fogbound corner,
A world of dead decorum, heavily haunted
By the charcoal spectres of Mr. Mantalini and Professor
    Turveydrop;
The fact that she had seen a whale
Washed up at Yarmouth;

And, strangest weight of all,
Her oft and loudly boasted declaration
That she had taken in the *Daily Mail*,
Each day since the *DAILY MAIL'S* beginning.

3. MISS MEW'S WINDOW-BOX

THE window-box, ever so high up,
Floating above the grey sea,
Crowded and clustered with brown, speeding wings
Was all the garden that Miss Mew possessed.
But this small coffin of earth
Was a whole world of life,
Flickered always with the brightly coloured buttons,
The sugar-sticks, rosettes, and candle-flames
Of early spring,
Or with the ragged cockscombs and the fuller bonfire-
flamings
Of the Autumn, trampling with its wild, golden hoofs:
For Miss Mew's calendar, just like her life,
Confessed to no high summer.

Over this oblong world,
Half-coconuts swung like hairy stars
In a miniature tarred gale from off the sea,
While cotton-wool-coated, coral-footed birds,
Acknowledging Miss Mew as feathery peer,
Pricked out a wooden music with their beaks,
Tapping against the various surfaces,
Or sent up little silver jets of song
Spurting against the crystal pane,
Or flew down on soft wings
With one soft wing quivering and bumping
Against her window, till she threw it up,

Her nimble fingers fluttering among the flowers,
Dispensing fruit and breadcrumbs.

.   .   .   .

But now the paint is off the window-box,
There come no flowers either in spring or autumn,
No sugar-sticks, rosettes or candle-flames,
No ragged cockscombs and no fuller bonfire-flamings.
The birds bump up against the window,
Staring like a vacant, bleary eye,
Bump wildly up against the window
As though they wished to fly in through the dark emptiness:
And warmly buried in the now flowerless earth
Where others lie so cold and still,
The worms wriggle and snigger at their triumph,
Now the nimble fingers are no more nimble,
And the silver thimble lies cold and tarnished black.

37   *Mrs. Kimber*

I. INVOCATION

A LL hail,
Ever borne back to mind
    On any salt and stinging wind
    That grows a rind
    Of tar!

All hail,
    Blythe spirit of the uncomplaining North
    (For such was Mrs. Kimber,
    Dear, dwindling Mrs. Kimber
    With her quick, crenellated smile
    And simple speech

That yet could never fail
In metaphor and image),
Yes, all hail, all hail!
See, she approaches;
There's her tartan shawl!
We must find a suitable accompaniment
For her appearance;
Let, then, no dancing, light-foot waves
Of southern seas, however azure-lined
And tipped with swansdown,
Their pale sands
Paven with pavonine and roseate shells
And parian limbs of gods and goddesses,
With cups of Bacchus and with ears of fauns,
Supply their trivial music for her.
But, instead, sound forth
Loud cacophonious breakers of the North,
Fringed with grey wings of seagulls,
Lined with black, slimy seaweed
And the bones of men.
You, too, you mournful bells,
Toll out from upright steeples
Of English seaside towns;
Sound your twin tongues,
St. Peter and St. Paul,
Toll out, St. Thomas and St. Saviour,
St. Ethelburga and St. John,
ALL,
ALL!

2. MRS. KIMBER

When the sea was smooth
—Hilly, that is, not mountainous—
Tolling bells could not depress her.

At night asleep,
And busy, very busy, all the day,
Bustling and dusting,
She was blythe and gay,
Singing like a kittiwake about her work
By the first light,
So greenly submarine,
That filtered in at frosty windows
—And this held equally at bay
The spectres of the past and future,
Spectres of the deep.
She lived, or seemed to live,
In an old house, so flashing white
It might be carved from salt,
That tilted down a hill,
Ribbed, herring-bone-like, with red tiles.
And here she tended
Her four stout sailor sons
      And darned and mended
        (Darned and mended).
Often away,
One upon each of the four seas,
She kept things ship-shape for them
    —Even when at home
    Life was conducted
    To the sound of bells,
    The very rhythm of the sea,
    While their rolling gait
    Brought the victorious rush of waters
    Into the timid, solid streets of houses.

Thus she was ever busy
On her sons' behalf,
Scrubbing floors,

Polishing glass-cases, kettles,
Washing doors,
Cutting spikes off urchins,
Whitewashing the yard
    —Where pointed jawbones of a whale or two
    Supplied triumphal arches for their valour;
    And wherein,
    Caught by her youngest,
    Flopped and flapped a seal,
    With the same sudden smile as Mrs. Kimber's.
'Like a cat for fish, that sea-calf',
    She would remark,
Applauding kindred zeal.

3. PROPERTIES AND PROSPECTS

THIS was her life, one thought
(Dear Mrs. Kimber, whose quick castellated smile
Still haunts me);
A busy life in rooms low-roofed,
Crowded with ostrich eggs, large spiky shells,
And coloured views of foreign parts
Prisoned in glass paper-weights,
And little ships in bottles.
Then there were ornaments of jet,
And, hanging on the wall,
The Queen, on her two jubilees
(Head resting on imperial hand),
Some brittle bunches of white seaweed
    By which to skill the weather,
And from each window
An abruptly falling street
Edged with wide seas;
While, as the prospect from the windows of her soul,

There stretched an acrid, waterproof perspective
Of fishing nets and bibles,
Red sails, red-herrings, kind tarpaulin faces,
All washed by a sea of soap-suds,
With Sunday as a weekly, workless culmination,
A formal day of dreams and how-d'you-dos,
Of boots like irons, violets in a bonnet,
And, just visible beyond this barrier,
Gigantic anti-climax of the usual Monday,
    Dim, workaday Monday
    Set in a golden cloud of whirling dust.

4. DAY DREAMS

BUT often
    (When the seas were smooth)
Mrs. Kimber was not there at all,
Floated out of her surroundings
Into an ideal world;
    A scaly universe, with Aberdeen,
    Distant and unattainable metropolis
    Of fishing nets and shawls,
    As its most fishy centre.
    She could almost hear them, almost smell them,
    Flopping alive upon the granite quays,
    Almost see them, wriggling mountains
    Of speckled gold and mottled silver, mostly silver,
    Emptied from the trawlers,
    To be appraised by expert eyes,
    And pinched by expert fingers.
Gleaming, writhing hills of herring, cod and codling,
Ling, sprat, in their season, sole, smelt and whiting,
Plaice, lait, dab, trout and salmon,
Gurnet, pennock, wuff and billet,

Thornback, Monk Fish (or Sea Devil),
Eels, conger eels and sand eels,
Cuttlefish, Black Jack and Old Fishwife.
'Fish', she would say, 'is in my very bones.'
>And so it was: she knew the names of them,
>So very many fishes,
>And their story,
>Their times and seasons,
>When to catch 'em, when to cook 'em
>(Almost, one felt, she comprehended their last
>>wishes),
>How the moon affected mackerel
>And the stars, a dory.

5. ROUGH WEATHER

BUT, when the sea was rough,
When the deep sound of bells
Was smothered in the gale
That cracked its whips
At every corner of the town,
When the thunder of the breakers
Pounded below, at cliff that crumbled,
Beneath the tearing cries of seagulls,
At once she'd quit her visionary world:
Then,
>Remembering her husband,
Her brain would turn all skimble-skamble,
And her eyes, flowers of the Northern waters,
Would strain toward the horizon,
Where the mountains shifted,
Watching, watching the seas wherein there sailed her
>sons;

Those Northern seas,
Lined with black, slimy seaweed
And the bones
Of men.
Toll from tall steeple,
Mournful bell!
But let
Your voice be caught, caught up and smothered in the wind,
So that it reach her not . . .
Not yet,
      Not yet.

6. COLOPHON

SEE how this stinging wind
Precipitates her in the mind,
A regular shape in crystal
Formed by the natural processes of chemistry!
See, there she sits now,
Beneath the ribboned portrait of her Queen!
Come, let us approach her:
We need fill
No beaker with the blushful Hippocrene,
But, while proud kettles puff their ostrich-plumes
And lids uprise upon a chanting gale,
From Indian herbs their sepia juice distil
And pledge her, crying again

        All hail,
           All hail!

BOOK III

SATIRES

Church-Parade

THE flattened sea is harsh and blue—
   Lies stiff beneath—one tone, one hue,
White concertina waves unfold
The painted shimmering sands of gold.

Each bird that whirls and wheels on high
Must strangle, stifle in, its cry,

For nothing that's of Nature born
Should seem so on the Sabbath morn.

The terrace glitters hard and white,
Bedaubed and flecked with points of light

That flicker at the passers-by—
Reproachful as a curate's eye.

And china flowers, in steel-bound beds,
Flare out in blues and flaming reds;

Each blossom, rich and opulent,
Stands like a soldier; and its scent

Is turned to camphor in the air.
No breath of wind would ever dare

To make the trees' plump branches sway,
Whose thick green leaves hang down to pray.

The stiff, tall churches vomit out
Their rustling masses of devout;

Tall churches whose stained Gothic night
Refuses to receive the light.

Watch how the stately walk along
Toward the terrace, join the throng

That paces carefully up and down
Above a cut-out cardboard town!

With prayer-book rigid in each hand,
They look below at sea and sand:

The round contentment in their eyes
Betrays their favourite fond surmise,

That all successful at a trade
Shall tread an eternal Church-Parade,

And every soul that's sleek and fat
Shall gain a heavenly top-hat.

From out the Church's Gothic night,
Past beds of blossoms china-bright,
Beneath the green trees' porous shade,
We watch the sea-side Church-Parade.

THE gilt-fring'd earth has sadly spun
 A sector of its lucent arc
About the disillusioned sun
Of Autumn. The bright angry spark

Of Heaven in each upturned eye
Denotes religious ecstasy.

We, too, have spun our Sunday round
Of Church and beef and after-sleep
In houses where obtrudes no sound
But breathing, regular and deep,

Till Sabbath sentiment, well-fed,
Demands a visit to the Dead.

For Autumn leaves sad thoughts beget,
As from life's tree they clatter down,
And Death has caught some in her net
Even on Sunday,—in this town,

Tho' money, food and sleep are sweet.
(The dead leaves rattle down the street.)

Fat bodies, silk-enmeshed, inflate
Their way along; if Death comes soon
They'll leave this food-sweet earth to float
Heavenward, like some huge balloon.

Religion dims each vacant eye
As we approach the cemet'ry.

Proudly we walk; with care we bend
To lead our children by the hand,
Here, where all, rich and poor, must end
—This portal to a better land

To which—if in good business—
We have hereditary access;

Where to afford the Saints relief
From prayer and from religious questions,
Round after round of deathless beef
Flatters celestial digestions:

Where, in white robe, with golden crown,
We watch our enemies sent down,

To other spheres, while we lean out,
Divinest pity in our eyes,
And wonder why these sinners flout
Our kindly pitying surprise,

Why look so angry when we play
On gold harps, as they go away,

A hymn tune, dear, familiar?
But now we stand within the space
Where marble females drape a tear
Above a whisker'd marble face.

'Isn't it pretty?' Even now
Rich and exotic blossoms grow

About each granite monument
Of men frock-coated, unaware
Of Judgment; what emolument
Requites a weeping willow's care?

Look!   Over there a broken column
Is watched by one geranium,

Whose scorching scarlet tones uphold
Damnation and eternal fire
To those who will not reckon gold—
Who are not worthy of their hire,

For marble tombs are prized above
Such brittle things as thought or love.

The crystal web of dusk now clings
From evergreen to tropic tree,
Toss'd by the wind that subtly brings
A mingled scent of mould and tea

That causes silence to be rent
By one scream—childish, but intent.

For children will not realize
That they should rest without a sound
With folded hands and downcast eyes
Here, in the Saint's Recruiting Ground.

And so, in sorrow, we turn back
To hasten on our high-tea track.

But after, in the night, we dream
Of Heaven as a marbled bank,
In which, in one continual stream,
We change our gold for heavenly rank,

Where each Saint, standing like a sentry,
Explains a mystic double-entry.

The Director of the Bank is God—
Stares our foes coldly in the face,
But gives us quite a friendly nod,
And beckons us to share His place.

40 *Au Bord de la Mer*

WHERE frightened woolly clouds, like sheep
    Scurry across blue skies; where sleep
Sings from the little waves that reach
In strict formation to the beach,
Are houses—covers of red-plush,
To hide our thoughts in, lest we blush.

.   .   .   .

Here live kind ladies.   Hence they come
To persecute us.   I am dumb
When they give from wide saucer-eye
Intolerable sympathy,
Or testify solicitude,
By platitude on platitude,
Mix Law-and-Order, Church-and-State
With little tales of Bishop Tait,
Or harass my afflicted soul
With most fantastic rigmarole
Of Bolshevik and Pope in league
With Jewish and Sinn-Fein intrigue.
I love to watch them, as they troop
Revolving, through each circus-hoop
Of new-laid eggs—left at the door
With Patriotism (for the Poor)—
Of ball-committee, Church Bazaar,
All leading up to a great war,

A new great war—greater by far
—Oh! much more great—than any war.

Kind lady, leave me, go enthral
The pauper-ward and hospital!

1919

Ultimate Judgment

WITHIN the sunny greenness of the close,
    Secure, a heavy breathing fell, then rose.
Here undulating chins sway to and fro,
As heavy blossoms do; the cheek's faint glow
Points to post-prandial port.   The willow weeps,
Hushed are the birds—in fact, the Bishop sleeps.

Then, suddenly, the wide sky blazes red!
Up from their graves arise the solemn dead,
The world is shaken; buildings fall in twain,
Exulting hills shout loud, then shout again
While, with the thunder of deep rolling drums
The angels sing.
                    At last Salvation comes.
The weak, the humble, the disdained, the poor
Are judged the first, and climb to Heaven's door.

    .   .   .   .

The Bishop wakes to see his palace crash
Down on the rocking ground—but in a flash
It dawns upon him.   With impressive frown,
He sees his second-housemaid in a crown,
In rainbow robes that glisten like a prism.
'I warned them . . .' said the Bishop—
        'Bolshevism!'

1919

ABOVE from plaster-mountains,
    Wine-shadowed by the sea,
Spurt white-wool clouds, as fountains
    Whirl from a rockery.

These clouds were surely given
    To keep the hills from harm,
For when a cloud is riven
    The fatted rain falls warm.

Through porous leaves the sun drops
    Each dripping stalactite
Of green.   The chiselled tree-tops
    Seem cut from malachite.

Stiff leaves with ragged edges
    (Each one a wooden sword)
Are carved to prickly hedges,
    On which, with one accord,

Their clock-work songs of calf-love
    Stout birds stop to recite,
From cages which the sun wove
    Of shade and latticed light.

Each brittle booth and joy-store
    Shines brightly.   Below these
The ocean at a toy shore
    Yaps like a Pekinese.

WHY do they sit in darkness,
   Hiss like geese?
Outside the sun flashes his strong wings
Against the green-slit shutters,
Through which you can see
Him bathing in the street.
Like a bird he preens himself at the windows,
Then dances back with the swimming flash of a gold-fish.
Why do you hiss like geese,
What do you hide,
With your thin sibilance of genteel speech?

   .   .   .   .

The Colonel, usually a rollicking character
In the manner of El Capitano,
Simpers, like any schoolgirl.
Miss Vera complains that her brother
Is suffering from catarrh.
On the other hand
Hotel-life is easier than home-life,
She just rings the bell,
Orders anything she wants,
—And there it is—punctual to the minute.
Both Sir William and his daughter
Are pleased with their holiday;
Admire the flora and the fauna;
Miss Ishmael sketches, and the place abounds
In peasants, picturesque old-bit-and-corner—

   .   .   .   .

If they should die . . .
Say only this of them,
That there's a corner in some foreign field

That is for ever England . . .
They travel; yet all foreign things
Are barr'd and bolted out of range
. . . While England benefits by the exchange.

Giardino Pubblico

Petunias in mass formation,
An angry rose, a hard carnation,
Hot yellow grass, a yellow palm
Rising, giraffe-like, into calm
—All these glare hotly in the sun.
Behind are woods, where shadows run
Like water through the dripping shade
That leaf and laughing wind have made.
Here silence, like a silver bird,
Pecks at the peach-ripe heat. . . . We heard
Townward, the voices, glazed with starch,
Of tourists on belated march
From church to church, to praise by rule
The beauties of the Tuscan School,
Clanging of trams, a hidden flute,
Sharp as the taste of unripe fruit;
Street organs join with tolling bell
To threaten us with both Heaven and Hell;
But through all taps a nearing sound
As of stage-horses pawing ground.
Then like a whale, confined in cage,
(In grandeur of a borrowed carriage)
The old Marchesa swims in sight
In tinkling jet that braves the light,

Making the sun hit out each tone
As if it played a xylophone,
Till she seems like a rainbow, where
She swells and, whale-like, spouts the air.

.   .   .   .

In passing, she imposed her will
Upon all things both live and still;
Lovers hid quickly—none withstood
That awful glance of widowhood;
Each child, each tree, the shrilling heat
Became encased in glacial jet;
The very songbird in the air
Was now a scarecrow dangling there,
While, if you turned to stare, you knew
The punishment Lot's wife went through.

.   .   .   .   .   .

Her crystal cage moves on.   Stagnation
Thaws once again to animation.
Gladly the world receives reprieve
Till six o'clock to-morrow eve,
When punctual as the sun, she'll drive
Life out of everything alive,
Then in gigantic glory, fade
Sunward, through the western glade. . . .

45   *English Gothic*

Aʙᴏᴠᴇ the valley drifts a fleet
Of white, small clouds.   Like castanets
The corn-crakes clack; down in the street
Old ladies air their canine pets.

The bells boom out with grumbling tone
To warn the people of the place
That soon they'll find upon His Throne
Their Maker, with a frowning face.

.   .   .   .   .

The souls of bishops, shut in stone
By masons, rest in quietude:
As flies in amber, they atone
Each buzzing long-dead platitude.

For lichen plants its golden flush
Here, where the gaiter should have bent;
With glossy wings the black crows brush
Carved mitres, caw in merriment.

Wings blacker than a verger's hat
Beat on the air.   These birds must learn
Their preaching note by pecking at
The lips of those who, treading fern,

Ascend the steps to Heaven's height.
—The willow herb, down by the wood,
Flares out to mark the phoenix-flight
Of God Apollo's car.   Its hood

Singes the trees.   The swans who float
—Wings whiter than the foam of sea—
Up the episcopal smooth moat,
Uncurl their necks to ring for tea.

.   .   .   .   .

At this sign, in the plump green close
The Deans say grace.   A hair pomade
Scents faded air.   But still outside
Stone bishops scale a stone façade.

A thousand strong, church-bound, they look
Across shrill meadows—but to find
The cricket bat defeats the Book
—Matter triumphant over Mind!

Wellington said Waterloo
Was won upon the playing-fields;
Which thought might comfort clergy who
Applaud the virtues that rank yields.

But prelates of stone cannot relate
An Iron Duke's strong and silent words.
The knights in armour rest in state
Within, and grasp their marble swords.

Above, where flutter angel-wings
Caught in the organ's rolling loom,
Hang in the air, like jugglers' rings,
Dim quatrefoils of coloured gloom.

Tall arches rise to imitate
The jaws of Jonah's whale.   Up flows
The chant.   Thin spinsters sibilate
Beneath a full-blown Gothic rose.

Pillars surge upward, break in spray
Upon the high and fretted roof;
But children scream outside—betray
The urging of a cloven hoof.

.   .   .   .   .   .

Tier above tier the Bishops stare
Away, away, . . . above the hills;
Their faded eyes repel the glare
Of dying sun, till sunset fills

Each pointed niche, in which they stand,
With glory of earth; humanity
Is spurned by one, with upturned hand,
Who warns them all is vanity.

The swan beneath the sunset arch
Expands his wings, as if to fly.
A thousand saints upon the march
Glow in the water—but to die.

A man upon the hill can hear
The organ.   Echoes he has found
That, having lost religious fear,
Are pagan; till the rushing sound

Clearly denotes Apollo's car,
That roars past moat and bridge and tree,
The Young God sighs. . . . How far, how far
Before the night shall set him free?

46   *Promenade*

LONG promenades against the sea
    Kaleidoscopic, chattering!
Pavilions rising from the sea,
On which a fawning, flattering,
Hot crush of Orientals move,
And sell their cheap and tawdry wares
To other Jews, and aldermen,
And rich, retired, provincial mayors.
Oh! many colours in the sun;
Copper and gold predominate!

Parasols, held 'gainst the sun
Throw down their shadows inchoate
On leering faces looking sly
And shining with the heat of June.
The shifting masses move and talk
And whistle tunes all out of tune.

Long promenades against the sea,
And oranges and mandolines!
Pavilions rising from the sea
And penny-in-the-slot machines!

47   *A Touch of Nature*

TRAINED to a charm of manner, to a smile
    —Enamelled and embalmed by Madame Rose
(Shame that an artist of this skill, this style,
Can never sign her work), no War-horse shows

Any emotion.   The poor Spartan Youth,
Though the fox gnawed his entrails, would not cry;
These never wince, nor hurl the mirror at Truth,
Though Old Age disembowel them secretly.

Throughout the day, blue shadows in the valley
Hover, crouch down, till dusk will let them rend
The last light on the hills; so wrinkles rally
To overwhelm these at their sudden end—

For Death strikes at the Old as well as Young,
And these—and these—may die at balls or races,
Or living death may make them loll the tongue,
Twitching in doll-like, hideous grimaces.

The very dab of rouge, that ghastly shred
Of self-respect, makes worse the look so winning
Of eyes—dead eyes, that know quite well they're dead—,
And yet retain a certain childish cunning.

And each day till the end, is dragged along
This painted bundle, trundled in its tomb,
Toward the sea where wondering children throng,
Mocked by this mask, this nodding lisp of doom

That almost apes them—save the open eye
Which contradicts the mouth, and knows the matter,
This terrible eye that moans 'I die, I die',
While the poor slobbering mouth can only chatter.

.   .   .   .

Then other War-horses pause, nod, go past,
—A few months younger these—and laugh together
(She, too, was hard and bold), nor note how fast
An egret's wing becomes a funeral feather.

They laugh and mutter, make their little jokes,
—And wonder if her lover had been bored—
'Look at the poor old thing!'
   The dumb voice chokes;
The eye is open yet—each word a sword!

BOOK IV

POEMS OF THE LAST AND THE NEXT WAR

INTRODUCTION

48 *How Shall We Rise to Greet the Dawn?*

How shall we rise to greet the dawn,
Not timidly,
With a hand before our eyes?

.   .   .   .

We will welcome the strong light
Joyfully:
Nor will we mistake the dawn
For the mid-day.

We must create and fashion a new God—
A God of power, of beauty, and of strength—
Created painfully, cruelly,
Labouring from the revulsion of men's minds.

It is not only that the money-changers
Ply their trade
Within the sacred places;
But that the old God
Has made the Stock Exchange his Temple.
We must drive him from it.
Why should we tinker with clay feet?

K*

We will fashion
A perfect unity
Of precious metals.

Let us tear the paper moon
From its empty dome.
Let us see the world with young eyes.
Let us harness the waves to make power,
And in so doing,
Seek not to spoil their rolling freedom,
But to endow
The soiled and straining cities
With the same splendour of strength.

We will not be afraid,
Though the golden geese cackle in the Capitol,
In fear
Lest their eggs may be placed
In an incubator.

.   .   .   .

Continually they cackle thus,
These venerable birds,
Crying, 'Those whom the Gods love
Die young'
Or something of that sort.
But we will see that they live
And prosper.

Let us prune the tree of language
Of its dead fruit.
Let us melt up the clichés
Into molten metal,

Fashion weapons that will scald and flay;
Let us curb this eternal humour
And become witty.
Let us dig up the dragon's teeth
From this fertile soil
Swiftly
Before they fructify;
Let us give them as medicine
To the writhing monster itself.

.   .   .   .

We must create and fashion a new God—
A God of power, of beauty, and of strength;
Created painfully, cruelly,
Labouring from the revulsion of men's minds.
Cast down the idols of a thousand years,
Crush them to dust
Beneath the dancing rhythm of our feet.
Oh! let us dance upon the weak and cruel:
We must create and fashion a new God.

November 1918

49 'Therefore is the Name of it called Babel'

AND still we stood and stared far down
Into that ember-glowing town,
Which every shaft and shock of fate
Had shorn unto its base.   Too late
   Came carelessly Serenity.

Now torn and broken houses gaze
On to the rat-infested maze
That once sent up rose-silver haze
   To mingle through eternity.

The outlines once so strongly wrought,
Of city walls, are now a thought
Or jest unto the dead who fought . . .
  Foundation for futurity.

The shimmering sands where once there played
Children with painted pail and spade,
Are drearly desolate—afraid
  To meet night's dark humanity,

Whose silver cool remakes the dead,
And lays no blame on any head
For all the havoc, fire, and lead,
  That fell upon us suddenly,

When all we came to know as good
Gave way to Evil's fiery flood,
And monstrous myths of iron and blood
  Seem to obscure God's clarity.

Deep sunk in sin, this tragic star
Sinks deeper still, and wages war
Against itself; strewn all the seas
With victims of a world disease
—And we are left to drink the lees
Of Babel's direful prophecy.

January 1916

50

The Eternal Club

To Roderick Meiklejohn

WARMING their withered hands, the dotards say:
    'In our youth men were happy till they died.
What is it ails the young men of to-day—
    To make them bitter and dissatisfied?'
Two thousand years ago it was the same:
    'Poor Joseph! How he'll feel about his son!
I knew him as a child—his head aflame
    With gold, he seemed so full of life and fun.
And even as a young man he was fine,
Converting tasteless water into wine. . . .
Then something altered him. He tried to chase
    The money-changers from the Temple door.
    White ringlets swung and tears shone in their poor
Aged eyes. He grew so bitter and found men
For friends as discontented—lost all count
    Of caste—denied his father, faith, and then
He preached that *dreadful* Sermon on the Mount!
    Nor even after, would he let things be;
    For when they nailed him high up on the tree,
And gave him vinegar, and pierced his side,
He asked God to forgive them—still dissatisfied!'

51

Arm-chair

IF I were now of handsome middle-age,
  I should not govern yet, but still should hope
To help the prosecution of this war.
I'd talk and eat (though not eat wheaten bread),
I'd send my sons, if old enough, to France,
Or help to do my share in other ways.

All through the long spring evenings, when the sun
Pursued its primrose path toward the hills,
If fine, I'd plant potatoes on the lawn;
If wet, write anxious letters to the Press.
I'd give up wine and spirits, and with pride
Refuse to eat meat more than once a day,
And seek to rob the workers of their beer.
The only way to win a hard-fought war
Is to annoy the people in small ways,
Bully or patronize them, as you will!
I'd teach poor mothers, who have seven sons
—All fighting men of clean and sober life—
How to look after babies and to cook;
Teach them to save their money and invest;
Not to bring children up in luxury
—But do without a nursemaid in the house!

If I were old or only seventy,
Then should I be a great man in his prime.
I should rule army corps; at my command
Men would rise up, salute me, and attack
—And die.   Or I might also govern men
By making speeches with my toothless jaws,
Constant in chatter, until men should say,
'One grand old man is till worth half his pay!'
That day, I'd send my grandsons out to France
—And wish I'd got ten other ones to send
(One cannot sacrifice too much, I'd say).
Then would I make a noble, toothless speech,
And all the list'ning Parliament would cheer.
'We cannot and we will not end this war
Till all the younger men with martial mien
Have enter'd capitals; never make peace
Till they are cripples, on one leg, or dead!'

Then would the Bishops go nigh mad with joy,
Cantuar, Ebor, and the other ones,
Be overwhelmed with pious ecstasy
In thanking Him we'd got a Christian,
An Englishman, still worth his salt, to talk.
In every pulpit would they preach and prance;
And our great Church would work, as heretofore,
To bring this poor old nation to its knees.
Then we'd forbid all liberty, and make
Free speech a relic of our impious past;
And when this war is finished, when the world
Is torn and bleeding, cut and bruised to death,
Then I'd pronounce my peace terms—to the poor!

.   .   .   .

But as it is, I am not ninety yet,
And so must pay my reverence to these men—
These grand old men, who still can see and talk,
Who sacrifice each other's sons each day.
O Lord!   let me be ninety yet, I pray.
Methuselah was quite a youngster when
He died.   Now, vainly weeping, we should say:
'Another great man perished in his prime!'
O let me govern, Lord, at ninety-nine!

August 1917

52   *The Trap*

THE world is young and green.
   Its woods are golden beneath the May-time sun;
But within its trap of steel the rabbit plunges
Madly to and fro.

It will bleed to death
Slowly,

  Slowly,
Unless there is some escape.
Why will not someone release it?

And presently a kindly passer-by
Stoops down.
The rabbit's eye glints at him—
Gleaming from the impenetrable obscurity of its prison.
He stoops and lifts the catch
(He cannot hold it long, for the spring is heavy).
The rabbit could now be free,
But does not move;
For from the darkness of its death-hutch
The world looks like another brightly baited trap.
So, remaining within its steel prison,
It argues thus:
  'Perhaps I may bleed to death,
  But it will probably take a long time,
  And, at any rate,
  I am secure
  From the clever people outside.
  Besides, if I did come out now
  All the people who thought I was a lion
  Would see, by the trap-mark on my leg,
  That I am only an unfortunate rabbit,
  And this might promote disloyalty among the children.

  . . . .

When the clamp closed on my leg
It was a ruse
To kill me,
So probably the lifting of it betrays the same purpose!

If I come out now
They will think they can trap rabbits
Whenever they like.
How do I know they will not snare me
Again next year?
Besides, it looks to me from here . . .'

But the catch drops down,
For the stranger is weary.
From within the hutch
A thin stream of blood
Trickles on to the grass
Outside,
And leaves a brown stain on its brightness.
But the dying rabbit is happy,
Saying:
'I knew it was only a trap!'

53   *Hymn to Moloch*

Holy Moloch, blessèd lord,
Hatred to our souls impart!
Put the heathen to the sword,
Wound and pierce each contrite heart
Never more shall darkness fall
But it seem a funeral pall;
Never shall the red sun rise
But to red and swollen eyes.
In the centuries that roll,
Slowly grinding out our tears,
Often Thou hast taken toll;
Never till these latter years
Have *all* nations lost the fray;
Lead not Thou our feet astray.

Never till the present time
Have we offered all we hold,
With one gesture, mad, sublime,
Sons and lovers, lands and gold.
Must we, then, still pray to Thee,
Moloch, for a victory?

Eternal Moloch, strong to slay,
Do not seek to heal or save.
Lord, it is the better way
Swift to send them to the grave.
Those of us too old to go
Send our sons to face the foe,
But, O lord! *we* must remain
Here, to pray and sort the slain.
In every land the widows weep,
In every land the children cry.
Other gods are lulled to sleep,
All the starving peoples die.
What is left to offer Thee?
Thou, O Sacred King of Death!
God of Blood and Lord of Guile,
Do not let us waste our breath,
Cast on us Thy crimson smile,
Moloch, lord, we pray to Thee,
Send at least *one* victory.

All the men in every land
Pray to Thee through battle's din,
Swiftly now to show thy hand,
Pray that soon one side may win.
Under sea and in the sky,
Everywhere our children die;
Laughter, happiness and light
Perished in a single night.

In every land the heaving tides
Wash the sands a dreadful red,
In every land the tired sun hides
Under heaps and hills of dead,
In spite of all we've offered up
Must we drink and drain the cup?
Everywhere the dark floods rise,
Everywhere our hearts are torn.
Every day a new Christ dies,
Every day a devil's born.
Moloch, lord, we pray to Thee,
Send at least *one* victory.

1917

54 *Old-Fashioned Sportsmen*

WE thank thee,
O Lord,
That the War is over.
We can now
Turn our attention
Again
To money-making.
Railway-Shares must go up;
Wages must come down;
Smoke shall come out
Of the chimneys of the North,
And we will manufacture battle-ships.

    We thank thee, O Lord,
    But we must refuse
    To consider
    Music, Painting, or Poetry.

Our sons and brothers
Went forth to fight,
To kill certain things,
Cubism, Futurism and Vers-libre.
    'All this Poetry-and-Rubbish,'
    We said,
    'Will not stand the test of war.'
We will not read a book
—Unless it is a best seller.
There has been enough art
In the past,
Life is concerned
With killing and maiming.
If they cannot kill men,
Why can't they kill animals?
There is still
Big Game in Africa
—Or there might be trouble
Among the natives.
    We thank thee, O Lord,
    But we will not read poetry

But as the Pharisees
Approached the tomb
They saw the boulder
Rolled back,
And that the tomb was empty.
—They said:
    'It's very disconcerting.
    I am not at all
    Narrow-minded.
    I know a tune
    When I hear one,

And I know
What I like—
I did not so much mind
That He blasphemed,
Saying that He was the Son-of-God,
But He was never, well,
What I call
A Sportsman;
For forty days
He went out into the desert
—And never shot anything:
And when we hoped He would drown,
He walked on the waters.'

55   *Corpse-Day*

                  (*July 19th*, 1919 *)

Dusk floated up from the earth beneath,
    Held in the arms of the evening wind
—The evening wind that softly creeps
Along the jasper terraces,
To bear with it
The old, sad scent
Of midsummer, of trees and flowers
Whose bell-shaped blossoms, shaken, torn
By the rough fingers of the day,
Ring out their frail and honeyed notes.

        .   .   .   .   .

Up from the earth there rose
Sounds of great triumph and rejoicing.

        .   .   .   .   .

            * The official celebration of Peace.
                    159

Our Lord Jesus, the Son of Man,
Smiled
And leant over the ramparts of Heaven.
Beneath Him
Through the welling clouds of darkness
He could see
The swarming of mighty crowds.

It was in the Christian Continent,
Especially,
That the people chanted
Hymns and pæans of joy.
But it seemed to Our Lord
That through the noisy cries of triumph
He could still detect
A bitter sobbing
—The continuous weeping of widows and children
Which had haunted Him for so long,
Though He saw only
The bonfires,
The arches of triumph,
The processions,
And the fireworks
That soared up
Through the darkening sky,
To fall in showers of flame
Upon the citadel of Heaven.
As a rocket burst,
There fell from it,
Screaming in horror,
Hundreds of men
Twisted into the likeness of animals
—Writhing men
Without feet,

Without legs,
Without arms,
Without faces. . . .

The earth-cities still rejoiced.
Old, fat men leant out to cheer
From bone-built palaces.
Gold flowed like blood
Through the streets;
Crowds became drunk
On liquor distilled from corpses.
And peering down
The Son of Man looked into the world;
He saw
That within the churches and the temples
His image had been set up;
But, from time to time,
Through twenty centuries,
The priests had touched up the countenance
So as to make war more easy
Or intimidate the people—
Until now the face
Had become the face of Moloch!
The people did not notice
The change
        . . . But Jesus wept!

56   *The Next War*

To SACHEVERELL

THE long war had ended.
  Its miseries had grown faded.
Deaf men became difficult to talk to,
Heroes became bores.

Those alchemists
Who had converted blood into gold
Had grown elderly.
But they held a meeting,
Saying,
'We think perhaps we ought
To put up tombs
Or erect altars
To those brave lads
Who were so willingly burnt,
Or blinded,
Or maimed,
Who lost all likeness to a living thing,
Or were blown to bleeding patches of flesh
For our sakes.
It would look well.
Or we might even educate the children.'
But the richest of these wizards
Coughed gently;
And he said:
        'I have always been to the front
        —In private enterprise—,
        I yield in public spirit
        To no man.
        I think yours is a very good idea
        —A capital idea—
        And not too costly. . . .
        But it seems to me
        That the cause for which we fought
        Is again endangered.
        What more fitting memorial for the fallen
        Than that their children
        Should fall for the same cause?'
Rushing eagerly into the street,

The kindly old gentlemen cried
To the young:
    'Will you sacrifice
    Through your lethargy
    What your fathers died to gain?
    The world *must* be made safe for the young!'

.   .   .   .

And the children
Went. . . .

November 1918